The Dynamics of Ch...

The Dynamics of China's Rejuvenation

Jianrong Huang

First published 2004 by
PALGRAVE MACMILLAN
Houndmills, Basingstoke, Hampshire RG21 6XS and
175 Fifth Avenue, New York, N.Y. 10010
Companies and representatives throughout the world

PALGRAVE MACMILLAN is the global academic imprint of the Palgrave
Macmillan division of St. Martin's Press, LLC and of Palgrave Macmillan Ltd.
Macmillan® is a registered trademark in the United States, United Kingdom
and other countries. Palgrave is a registered trademark in the European
Union and other countries.

ISBN 0–333–92051–1

This book is printed on paper suitable for recycling and made from fully
managed and sustained forest sources.

A catalogue record for this book is available from the British Library.

Library of Congress Cataloging-in-Publication Data
Huang, Jianrong.
    The dynamics of China's rejuvenation / Jianrong Huang.
        p. cm.
    Includes bibliographical references and index.
    ISBN 0–333–92051–1
    1. China—Economic policy—1976–2000. 2. China—Economic
    Policy—2000– 3. China—Politics and government—1976– I. Title.
    HC427.92.H827 2004
    338.951—dc22
                                                        2003060851

10   9   8   7   6   5   4   3   2   1
13 12 11 10 09 08 07 06 05 04

Printed and bound in Great Britain by
Antony Rowe Ltd, Chippenham and Eastbourne

In memory of my parents

Contents

List of Figures and Tables   ix

Preface and Acknowledgements   xi

List of Abbreviations   xiii

1 **Introduction**   1

   China's growing eminence in the world   2
   Historical background   2
   The structure of the book   7

2 **China's Rejuvenation**   9

   China's epoch-making development   10
   International responses to China's rejuvenation   17

3 **The Part Played by Chinese People in Bringing
   About Reforms**   21

   Intellectuals as pioneers in pushing forward social change   21
   The part played by officers in political and
      institutional change   26
   The part played by ordinary people in bringing
      about change   30
   The part played by collective action   33
   Li Rui and his proposal for reform of the political system   38

4 **The Part Played by Chinese Leaders Since 1978**   41

   The selection of Deng Xiaoping as paramount leader   41
   The redressing of past social and political wrongs   44
   The unswerving adherence to the central task of
      economic construction   47
   The unswerving pursuit of reforms and opening up   49
   Conclusion   56

5   **The Key Role of Deng Xiaoping**   59

Deng's main contributions to China's rejuvenation   60
How was Deng able to make such remarkable
   contributions to China's rejuvenation?   70

6   **The Fundamental Impetus Provided by the
   Chinese National Spirit**   75

The spirit of self-improvement   76
The spirit of humanity   77
The spirit of diligence   77
The spirit of exploration   78
The spirit of creativity   78
The spirit of moral integrity   79
The spirit of patriotism   79
The spirit of revolution   80
The spirit of reform   81
The spirit of opening up to the outside world   81

7   **The Momentum that Stemmed from Globalisation**   83

8   **The Dynamics of China's Future Development**   89

China's rapidly strengthening economic power as
   the basis of further development   89
The backing of the people   91
The stable transfer of power   91
The experiences learnt from China's reform practices   92
A clearly defined target for living standards   94
Ideological emancipation   95
Membership of the World Trade Organization   96
The international environment   98

Notes   101

References   109

Index   115

List of Figures and Tables

Figures

2.1 Growth of China's GDP, 1952–2002   11
2.2 Household consumption, China, 1978–2001   16
7.1 Share of world manufacturing production,
    major producers, 1750–1980   85

Tables

2.1 Average annual increase in GDP, selected
    countries, 1980–98   11
2.2 The world's top ten economies, 2001   12
2.3 Economic performance of the major transition
    economies and developing countries, 1980–98   13
2.4 Changing rankings of the main industrial
    products output in the world, China, 1949–2000   14
2.5 Changing rankings of the main agricultural
    products output in the world, China, 1949–2001   15
2.6 Changes in the Engel coefficient, China, 1954–2000   16
2.7 GDP growth, China, the United States and
    Japan, 1994–2015   18
4.1 The share of state-owned, collectively owned and
    privately owned enterprises in GDP, 1978–96   51
4.2 The share of state-owned, collectively owned and
    privately owned industrial enterprises in gross
    output, 1978–97   51
4.3 Agricultural yields, major crops, 1978–99   52
4.4 Per capita income, rural households, 1980–2002   52
4.5 Foreign investment in China, 1979–2002   56
7.1 Per capita GNP and GDP annual growth rate, selected
    Asian countries, and regions, 1960–78   86
8.1 Predicted growth of GDP, China, 2000–29   90

Preface and Acknowledgements

This book examines the main reasons for and driving forces behind China's epoch-making rejuvenation since 1979, including the desires of and impulses from the people, the role of the paramount leader, the impetus provided by China's leaders adhering to the reforms, the impact of the Chinese national spirit and the momentum of globalisation. The dynamics of China's future development is also investigated.

I started writing this book in late 1999 when I was conducting research at the University of Newcastle. However, due to my heavy workload in the UK and after taking up a professorship at Nanjing University at the end of 2000, this work was not completed as quickly as expected. Accordingly I am very grateful to Amanda Watkins of Palgrave Macmillan for encouraging me to continue writing and her tolerance of delays. I also wish to thank Tim Farmiloe, Dominic Knight, Tim Gough and Kerry Coutts for their support and help with preparing the manuscript.

My thanks also go to Jie Qian, my postgraduate student, for preparing some of the tables and figures in the book; Hai Zhou, a student at Queen Mary College, London University, for his help in collecting data; and MacLean Brodie, my Canadian student, for modifying the English in some of the chapters.

Finally, I am particularly grateful to Susan Jiang, my wife, for her support, tolerance and the space she gave me to get on with my work; and Jia, my son, for making such an effort with his university studies, which has made me happy and given impetus to my writing.

December 2003   JIANRONG HUANG

List of Abbreviations

CCYL	Chinese Communist Youth League
CMC	Central Military Commission
CPC	Communist Party of China
CPPCC	Chinese People's Political Consultative Conference
FDI	Foreign Direct Investment
IEP	Index of Economic Power
IMD	Lausanne Institute of International Management and Development
KMT	Kuomingtang
NPC	National People's Congress
PLA	People's Liberation Army
PRC	People's Republic of China
SEZ	Special Economic Zone
WEF	World Economic Forum

1
Introduction

The dawn of the twenty-first century marked the rejuvenation of the Chinese nation. China not only made a successful bid to host the Olympic Games in 2008 but also joined the WTO and hosted an APEC Conference for the first time. Moreover, in 2002 it became the top country in the world for foreign direct investment, reflecting its great attractiveness to investors and potential for further development. In 2003, China's Shenzhou 5 spacecraft was successfully launched and returned to ground safely, making China the third nation in the world to send a man into space, and indicating China's comprehensive strength of science and technology.

The goal of building a prosperous society with a higher standard of living for all was placed high on the agenda of the Communist Party of China (CPC) in November 2002. Fifty-four years ago, Mao Zedong prophesied that one day China would stand on an equal footing with the rest of the world, and today this is becoming a reality. With the rapid burgeoning of the economy, China is playing an increasingly important part in international affairs and the Chinese people have not felt so fulfilled or content since the mid-nineteenth century.

Over the last two decades economic development has proceeded with breathtaking speed and there has been remarkable social change. This progress has far-reaching significance in that it is showing the world that China is capable of realizing national rejuvenation after nearly two hundred years of stagnation and slow development. How has China been able to bring about so many outstanding achievements in such a short time? What are the fundamental dynamics behind these achievements? What are the likely effects of the rise of

1

China? These issues have attracted broad attention and international research interest. This book explores the causal dynamics of China's rejuvenation in order not only to aid understanding of China's current and future development but also to show other countries that lag behind the industrialised world that they too can rejuvenate their economies.

China's growing eminence in the world

In the process of economic development China is aiming to build a well-off society with higher all-round standards and a thriving market economy. Three particular features of China's recent development have captured international attention. First, of the countries with a long history of civilisation, China is the only one to recover its economic and social vitality with such extraordinary speed. Second, among the developing countries China has been most successful at sustaining rapid economic growth. Third, among the countries in transition from a centrally planned to a market economy, China has proved best at facilitating reforms in the interest of economic development. In short, no country in these three groups has been able to match China's performance over the past quarter of a century.

Historical background

Despite China's long and remarkable history of civilisation, in the middle of the nineteenth century it began to lag behind the industrialising countries and later reached an all-time low in terms of development. Without knowledge of China's early achievements and its miserable history since the Opium War, it is not possible to understand fully the significance of its recent rejuvenation. Therefore, it is essential to provide a brief history.

China is one of the world's most ancient civilisations, together with ancient Egypt, Babylon and India, and its written historical records go back nearly 4000 years. It is not only one of the cradles of the human race but also the only ancient civilisation to continue to this day. Fossils found in Chinese territory include those of Yuanmou man, the first *Homo erectus*, who lived 1.7 million years ago, Lantian man, who lived 750 000 years ago, and Peking man, who lived in

Zhoukoudian (today's suburban Beijing) 600 000 years ago. Fossils of the Shu ape, a primate that lived 45 million years ago and is known as the first anthropoid, were discovered in China in 1994.

The birth of Chinese civilisation took place some 7000 to 8000 years ago, as revealed by archaeological evidence of the Daxi culture in Sichuan and Hubei provinces, the Majiapang culture in Jiangsu and Zhejiang provinces, the Hemudu culture in eastern Zhejiang and the Yangshou culture along the middle reaches of the Yellow River and its main tributaries. According to legend, the numerous primitive tribes that inhabited the middle and upper reaches of the Yellow River were unified into two powerful tribes under the Yellow Emperor and the Fiery Emperor. Some 5000 years ago they began to push southward, and after many years of warfare they conquered the Sanmiao and Jiuli tribes in southern China. Some members of the defeated tribes were incorporated into the conquering tribes to become a part of the Han people, thus marking the beginning of the Chinese nation. Nowadays Chinese people often refer to themselves as 'descendants of the Yellow and Fiery Emperors'.[1]

According to archaeological studies, approximately 5000 years ago China became a patriarchal society. Villages and then cities began to appear, and there is evidence that the population had already reached a fairly large size and agriculture had made great headway. Many important discoveries occurred during this period. An individual named Shen Nong sought out and tasted various wild plants, some of which were selected for cultivation as food and herbal medicines. The Yellow Emperor invented the compass, which helped him on his journey to defeat Chi You, the leader of the southern tribes. The appearance of wheeled carts greatly reduced the need for labourers. Lei Su, wife of the Yellow Emperor, discovered that the fibre made by silkworms could be used to produce garments, which allowed people to bid goodbye to the wearing of animal skins and other makeshift clothing. Tribespeople in the south learned how to make weapons from copper, thus paving the way for the metallurgy of later times.[2]

The Xia Dynasty (2100–1600 BC) marked the arrival of slavery and the Shang Dynasty (1600–1100 BC) saw the height of bronze culture, with new smelting and casting techniques allowing the production of watertight vessels. The art of pottery developed very rapidly, and sericulture and silk weaving reached maturity. In about 475 BC China entered a long feudal period. By the fifteenth century China was one of the most powerful countries in the world and it led in terms of agriculture, irrigation, technology, ceramics, textiles, metallurgy, medicine and botanical knowledge. China's four greatest inventions – the compass, gunpowder, movable type printing and papermaking – accelerated the evolution of modern civilisation.

China also produced the world's earliest and most detailed astronomical records as well as the most advanced astronomical apparatus. In the field of thought, Confucianism had far-reaching significance not only for China but also for the rest of East and South-East Asia. Moreover the strategies introduced by the noted military strategist Sun Zi are still studied and referred to today. Taoism, which later became a sole independently established Chinese religion, was an important school of thought. Its advocacy of 'quietude and inaction' echoes in the thoughts of many people today.

In short, and as pointed out by Joseph Needham, an eminent sinologist and the world's top authority on Chinese science and technology, China was way ahead of the West in terms of civilisation and almost every area of science and technology from early times to the Middle Ages.

Unfortunately China's feudal political and bureaucratic systems gradually became rigid and lacking in vitality, which halted the progress of science, technical innovation, thinking and culture. This inevitably led to a decline in productivity and caused China to lose importance later in the eyes of the rest of the world.

In the nineteenth century China was plagued by disasters, including the two Opium Wars. Early in the century Britain started to smuggle in large quantities of opium, the sale of which caused a large outpouring of Chinese silver and severe economic disruption. In 1839 Lin Zexu, a government commissioner, was sent to Guangdong to enforce a prohibition on opium trafficking. In retaliation, in 1840 Britain initiated the First Opium War and the Chinese people rose in armed struggle under the leadership of Lin Zexu and other generals. However, the corrupt and incompetent Qing government capitulated to the invaders. With the signing of the humiliatory Treaty of Nanjing, it agreed to the cession of Hong Kong to Britain and the opening of five treaty ports for the conduct of foreign trade. Following that, China was gradually turned into a semi-colonial and semi-feudal country.

In the subsequent years China's situation continued to deteriorate. Between 1840 to 1949 Britain, the United States, France, Russia, and Japan forced China to sign various unequal treaties by waging numerous wars of varying intensity, and even seized 'concessions' that divided parts of China into 'spheres of influence'. The aggression of imperialism and the oppression of feudalism and bureaucratic capitalism caused untold misery and countless deaths through war and famine. In 1900, following the Boxer uprising, troops from eight Allied Powers – Germany, Japan, Britain, Russia, France, the United States, Italy and Austria systematically killed, burned and looted. Tanggu, a town of 50 000 residents, was reduced to ruins, the population of Tianjin was reduced from one million to 100 000, and countless people were killed when troops entered Beijing, with more than 1700 being slaughtered in Zhuangwangfu alone.

The imperialists also sold and mistreated numerous Chinese labourers. According to some statistics, more than 12 million indentured Chinese labourers were sold to various parts of the world between the mid-1800s and the 1920s. Once abducted, these labourers were thrown into lockups known as 'pigsties', where they were branded with the names of the destinations allotted to them. During 1852–58, 40 000 people were put into such pigsties in Shantou alone, and more than 8000 died there. Equally horrifying was the death of ill-treated labourers in factories and mines run by imperialists across China.

During Japan's full-scale war of aggression against China, which began in 1937, more than 21 million people were killed or wounded and another 10 million were persecuted or tortured to death.[3] After the fall of Nanjing the invaders went on a rampage of killing, raping and looting that lasted six weeks. Over 300 000 Chinese civilians and soldiers were massacred and one third of the houses in the city were burnt to the ground.[4] During the Japanese occupation no fewer than two million factory and mine labourers perished from maltreatment and exhaustion in north-east China. Their bodies were thrown into mountain gullies or pits dug into hillsides. More than 80 massive pits have since been excavated and over 700 000 skeletons found.

Under the various periods of foreign occupation the Chinese people had no personal dignity to speak of, as exemplified in 1885 by a sign at the entrance of a park in the French concession that read 'Chinese and dogs not admitted'. The occupiers exercised administrative, legislative, judicial and financial power in their 'concessions', thus turning them into 'states within a state' that were thoroughly independent of China's administrative and legal systems. With more than 1100 unequal treaties that were forced on China the occupiers plundered the country's wealth on a huge scale. Records show that more than 100 billion taels of silver[5] were lost by China over the years. Nearly two million taels were extorted through the Sino-British Treaty of Nanjing, the Sino-Japanese Treaty of Shimonoseki, the International Protocol of 1901 and five other such treaties, 16 times the 1901 revenue of the Qing government. The Treaty of Shimonoseki earned Japan 230 million taels in extortion money, about four and a half times its annual national revenue. Moreover incalculable losses were incurred from the destruction and looting carried out by invading troops. It is estimated that the Japanese invasion and occupation of 930 Chinese cities resulted in US$62 billion of direct losses and US$500 billion of indirect losses.

With their state sovereignty impaired, their social wealth plundered or destroyed, and deprivation of their basic necessities for survival, over the years the Chinese people pursued unrelenting struggles for national independence and people's liberation. The Taiping Heavenly Kingdom Movement, the Boxer Movement and the Revolution of 1911, which overthrew the Qing Dynasty, arose during this period and dealt a heavy blow to imperialist influences. However, fundamental change took place only after the Chinese people, under the leadership of the Chinese Communist Party, overthrew the Kuomintang rulers and founded the People's Republic of China in 1949.

From the time of its birth in 1921, the Communist Party's primary goals were to achieve complete independence for the Chinese nation and to unite China into a real democratic republic with sufficient food and warm clothing for all. Nevertheless, in those days before 1949, successive regimes in old China brought even more disasters to the people. The old China was a society in which most of the people were cruelly exploited and oppressed. For example, landlords and rich peasants accounted for just 10 per cent of the rural population but held 70 per cent of the land. In the meantime the bureaucrat-comprador bourgeoisie, who made up only a small fraction of the population, monopolised 80 per cent of industrial capital and controlled the economic lifelines of the country. Ordinary Chinese people were continuously exploited and the poverty they suffered was of a degree rarely seen in other parts of the world. According to 1932 statistics, Chinese peasants were subject to 1656 types of taxes and levies that took away 60–90 per cent of their harvests. Their lives were made all the more miserable by corrupt and impotent governments that surrendered China's sovereign rights to foreign imperialists, and by separatist warlords embroiled in endless wars. It was estimated that 80 per cent of the population suffered from varying degrees of starvation and malnutrition and tens of thousands – hundreds of thousands in some cases – died of it every year. Major natural disasters and famines invariably left the land strewn with the corpses of victims. More than 3.7 million lives were lost when floods hit eastern China in 1931. In 1943, a crop failure in Henan Province resulted in the death of three million people and 15 million were forced to subsist on grass and bark, all the while struggling on the verge of death. After victory in the war of resistance against Japan, renewed civil war caused total economic collapse. In 1946, 10 million people died of hunger. The next year 100 million, or 22 per cent of the population, were under the constant threat of death from malnutrition.[6]

After more than a century of bloody struggle the Chinese people were at last liberated and won independence with the founding of the People's Republic, which put an end to the humiliation and oppression associated with imperialism, feudalism and bureaucratic-capitalism. Thus China became free to build a prosperous and strong socialist society. After twenty-odd years of experimenting with various types of reform to promote economic and social development, it was decided that the best way forward would be to reform economic and political systems, and open up the country to the outside world, integrate China into the global economy and engage in international competition on equal terms. A range of new policies and measures brought about miraculous economic growth and social change within the relatively short period of 20 years, thus rejuvenating the Chinese nation.

The structure of the book

How did China begin its rejuvenation? What were the main impetuses? Why does China's development stand out from those of other developing countries and countries in transition? To answer these questions, this book will analyse the internal and external dynamics of China's rejuvenation.

Chapter 2 discusses the major achievements of the reform and opening-up processes. Chapter 3 explores the part played in this by ordinary Chinese people, and shows that it was their demands and pressures that provided the impetus for change. Chapter 4 assesses the work of China's leading group in promoting modernisation, and its firm adherence to the reform targets. Chapter 5 discusses the particular contribution made by Deng Xiaoping, who was China's pre-eminent leader from the end of the 1970s to the mid-1990s and who played a very important role in state affairs and the introduction of economic reforms. Chapter 6 looks at how the Chinese national spirit spurred the efforts to bring about a better future. Chapter 7 examines the impact of globalisation and the external dynamics of China's rejuvenation. Finally, Chapter 8 considers the country's future development and analyses the conditions needed to sustain China's growth.

2
China's Rejuvenation

China's miraculous economic growth and social development since the late 1970s has surprised the world. No matter how many short-comings and problems remain, nobody can deny the remarkable progress made by China after almost two centuries of stagnation and backwardness.

While the UN, the IMF and other organizations were lowering their estimates of world economic growth, in light of the continuing global recession, international business figures and political leaders who attended the 2003 World Economic Forum in Davos, Switzerland, voiced their opinion that China was likely to become an important engine of world economic growth because it was one of the few bright points in the world economy.[1] Indeed, while many countries have succumbed to recession, China's growth rate has remained strong, reaching 8 per cent in 2002. In the same year China became the top country in the world for direct foreign investment, attracting $52 billion of inflows. Gail Fosler, chief economist of the World's Association of Big Enterprises, even predicted that China's economic strength would exceed that of Europe in 10 or 15 years.[2]

In 1949, when the People's Republic was founded, China was one of the poorest countries in the world. According to UN statistics, per capita income was just $27 US dollars, compared with $57 for India and $44 for Asia as a whole. After 50 odd years, great changes have taken place. According to *Le Figaro* of France, 50 per cent of the world's camcorders, 30 per cent of televisions and air-conditioners, 25 per cent of washing machines and 20 per cent of refrigerators now bear the label 'Made in China'.[3] *The Economy Weekly* of Germany also marvels at the momentum of China's development: 'In 1988 China's GDP was only half that of Russia, but after ten years the situation had reversed. Twenty years ago China's per capita GDP was the same as India's, but now it is double that of India.'[4]

Thus, experts such as Frank Jürgen Richter, Director of the World Economic Forum, suggest that Western countries should change their views about China. Richter points out that

> as a member of Group 8, Italy's total GDP amount is incomparable with that of China staying outside the Group... this is the most important index... if Group 8 wants to be representative in the world, it should not neglect the existence of China. Of course, involved here are not only economic factors, but also political factors. More and more people have recognized the importance of China's economic development; Western countries should treat China as an equal partner as soon as possible.

He particularly stresses that China is likely to replace the United States as the engine of world economic growth.[5] Obviously Richter's comments point to the importance of China's sustained and speedy development and its impact on the rest of the world.

China's epoch-making development

From the outset of the reforms and with clearly defined targets in place, the Chinese people worked as one to score an achievement step by step. By 2001, GDP had reached 9.6 trillion yuan ($1.16 trillion), almost three times that of 1989 and representing an average annual increase of 9.3 per cent. Moreover, China came sixth in the world in terms of economic aggregate. During the process the people moved from having only adequate food and clothing to leading a prosperous life.[6]

Between 1979 and 1988, the average annual economic growth rate was 10.1 per cent, compared with 2.7 per cent for developed countries and 3.4 per cent for developing countries. In 1989–97, the figures were 9.5 per cent, 2.2 per cent and 3.2 per cent respectively.[7] In 1998–99, although strongly affected by the Asian financial crisis, China's economic growth rate still reached 7.15 per cent. Throughout the period 1980–98, the growth of the Chinese economy outstripped

those of the other Asian economies (Table 2.1). In 2002, GDP stood at
10.2 trillion yuan, more than 28 times that of 1978 and more than
150 times that of 1952[8] (Figure 2.1). In 2001, China's GDP ranked sixth
in the world in exchange rate terms and second in terms of purchasing
power parity, second only to the United States[9] (Table 2.2). Obviously,
China's extraordinary economic achievements deserve a prominent
place in the annals of the late twentieth century.

Compared with other countries in transition to a market economy,
China's economic growth is remarkable. According to the World
Bank the 28 transition economies can be divided into four groups

Table 2.1 Average annual increase in GDP, selected
countries, 1980–98 (per cent)

	1980–90	*1990–98*
China	10.2	11.1
Singapore	6.6	8.0
Vietnam	4.6	8.6
Thailand	7.6	7.4
Malaysia	5.5	7.7
Lebanon	n.a.	7.7
South Korea	9.4	6.2
Indonesia	6.1	5.8
World	3.2	2.4

Source: World Bank (1999), pp. 256–7.

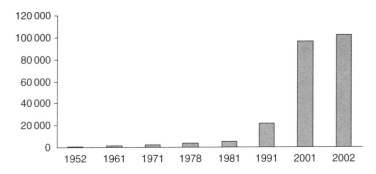

Figure 2.1 Growth of China's GDP, 1952–2002 (100 million yuan)*
*Data calculated at current prices.
Source: *China Statistical Yearbook* (2002), p. 51.

Table 2.2   The world's top ten economies, 2001

	GDP ($ bn)	Rank		GDP (PPP, $ bn)	Rank
United States	9837.4	1	United States	9601	1
Japan	4841.6	2	China	4951	2
Germany	1873.0	3	Japan	3436	3
United Kingdom	1414.6	4	India	2375	4
France	1294.2	5	Germany	2047	5
China	1079.9	6	France	1438	6
Italy	1074.0	7	United Kingdom	1407	7
Canada	687.9	8	Italy	1354	8
Brazil	595.5	9	Brazil	1243	9
Mexico	574.5	10	Russia	1165	10

Source: The Economist (2002), p. 25.

based on labour productivity in industry. Group 1 consists of those countries whose economies recovered after an initial decline and now exceed their performance level before the reform. These countries include Poland, Hungary and Slovenia. Group 2 comprises those economies that are in the process of recovering but have not yet reached their pre-reform level, including Romania, Croatia, Bulgaria and the Czech Republic. Group 3 consists of economies that are still failing. Finally, group 4 consists of economies that have enjoyed positive growth from the start. China stands at the top not only of this group[10] but also of the group of major developing countries with similar economic backgrounds (Table 2.3).

If we examine China's record in more detail, we can see that it has performed outstandingly in the following areas:[11]

- Economic growth: since the 1980s, China has had the fastest economic growth in the world, with an average annual increase of 9.4 per cent.
- Foreign trade increase: in 1978, China's imports and exports amounted to $20.6 billion and China ranked twenty seventh in the world. By 2001, this figure had increased to $509.8 billion (a rise of almost 2400 per cent) and China ranked sixth in the world.

Table 2.3 Economic performance of the major transition economies and developing countries, 1980–98 (average growth per annum, per cent)

	GDP		Agricultural value added		Industrial value added		Services value added		Exports of goods and services	
	1980–90	1990–98	1980–90	1990–98	1980–90	1990–98	1980–90	1990–98	1980–90	1990–98
Transition economies										
China	10.2	11.1	5.9	4.3	11.1	15.4	13.7	9.3	11.5	14.9
Vietnam	4.6	8.6	4.3	5.1	n.a.	13.3	n.a.	8.8	n.a.	27.7
Poland	1.8	4.5	-0.7	-0.6	-1.3	4.7	2.8	3.0	4.5	12.3
Mongolia	5.4	0.1	1.4	1.9	6.7	-2.0	5.8	1.2	n.a.	n.a.
Czech Republic	1.7	-0.2	n.a.	n.a.	n.a.	n.a.	n.a.	n.a.	n.a.	7.0
Hungary	1.3	-0.2	1.7	3.8	0.2	1.1	2.1	0.3	3.6	4.9
Russia	n.a.	-7.0	n.a.	-6.9	n.a.	-8.1	n.a.	-4.7	n.a.	2.0
Ukraine	n.a.	-13.1	n.a.	-21.4	n.a.	-16.4	n.a.	-8.6	n.a.	-3.2
Developing countries										
China	10.2	11.1	5.9	4.3	11.1	15.4	13.7	9.3	11.5	14.9
India	5.8	6.1	3.1	3.4	7.0	6.7	6.9	7.9	5.9	12.4
Indonesia	6.1	5.8	3.4	2.8	6.9	9.9	7.0	7.2	2.9	8.6
Sri Lanka	4.0	5.3	2.2	1.5	4.6	6.5	4.7	6.3	4.9	9.0
Pakistan	6.3	4.1	4.3	3.8	7.3	5.0	6.8	4.6	8.4	3.2
Brazil	2.7	3.3	2.8	3.1	2.0	3.2	3.3	3.3	7.5	5.6
Mexico	0.7	2.5	0.8	1.4	1.1	3.2	0.6	2.4	7.0	14.7

Source: World Bank (1999), pp. 250–1.

- Foreign exchange reserves: in 1978, China's foreign exchange reserves amounted to $0.167 billion. Today, they stand at $250 billion and China ranks second in the world.

- Production growth: by 1996, China's total output of crude steel had reached 100 million tons and China overtook Japan to become the top producer. It is also the top producer of other important industrial and agricultural products, such as televisions, fertilisers, cereals and processed cotton (see Tables 2.4 and 2.5 for the changing rankings of industrial and agricultural products).

- Foreign direct investment: prior to the reforms, foreign investment in China was almost zero but, in 2002, direct foreign investment amounted to $52 billion, the highest FDI investment rate in the world.

According to the facts shown above, it is conceivable that China has entered a period of miraculous economic growth since the end of 1970s. Thus, now China's comprehensive state power has strengthened greatly, the people's living standard has improved tremendously, and China's status in international community has grown steadily. As indicated by the 'Report on the 2002–2003 Global

Table 2.4 Changing rankings of the main industrial products output in the world, China, 1949–2000

	1949	1978	1980	1985	1990	1995	1999	2000[1]
Crude steel	26	5	5	4	4	2	1	1
Coal	9	3	3	2	1	1	1	1
Crude petroleum	27[2]	8	6	6	5	5	5	5
Electricity	25	7	6	5	4	2	2	2
Cement	–	4	4	1	1	1	1	1
Fertilisers	–	3	3	3	3	2	1	1
Chemical fibres	–	7	5	4	2	2	2	2
Woven cotton fabrics	–	1	1	1	1	1	2	2
Sugar	–	8	10	6	6	4	3	3
Televisions	–	8	5	3	1	1	1	1

Notes:
1. Estimated.
2. Data refer to 1950.
Source: China Statistical Yearbook (2002), p. 932.

Table 2.5   Changing rankings of the main agricultural products output in the world, China, 1949–2001

	1949	1978	1980	1985	1990	1995	2000	2001
Cereals	–	2	1	2	1	1	1	1
Meat*	3	3	3	2	1	1	1	1
Cotton lint	4	3	2	1	1	1	1	1
Soybeans	2	3	3	3	3	3	4	4
Groundnuts in shell	2	2	2	2	2	1	1	1
Rapeseeds	2	2	2	1	1	1	1	1
Sugar cane	–	9	9	4	4	3	3	3
Tea	3	2	2	2	2	2	2	2
Fruit	–	–	10	8	4	1	1	1

*Data refer to pork, beef and mutton prior to 1993.
Source: China Statistical Yearbook (2002), p. 932.

competitiveness' released by the World Economic Forum, China's economic competitiveness further rose by six places in 2003.[12]

To further observe and analyse China's economic growth and social development, we can see more in details from the enormous improvement of people's living quality. For example, the income of urban and rural residents has gone up steadily, and their standard of living has continued to improve. The Chinese people nationwide have jumped from the stage of having enough to eat and wear to that of living a better-off life. In 2000, the disposable income per urban resident came to 6280 Yuan, or an increase of 6.4 per cent over that of the previous year, in real terms; the net income per rural resident reached 2253 Yuan, or a growth of 2.1 per cent over that of the previous year, in real terms. During the Ninth Five-Year Plan period (1996–2000), savings deposits of urban and rural residents more than doubled and, by 2000, had topped 6400 billion Yuan, or an increase of more than five times compared to that of eight years previously.[13] The consumption level has been constantly improved over the last two decades, which indicates that real achievement stemmed from China's reform and development (see Figures 2.1 and 2.2)

Household consumption has soared since 1978 (Figure 2.2) and the general standard of living has improved considerably. Statistics show that the structure of consumption has been optimised: the proportion

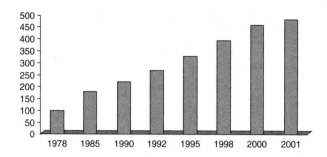

Figure 2.2   Household consumption, China, 1978–2001 (index, 1978 = 100)
Note: Indices are calculated at comparable prices.
Source: *China Statistical Yearbook* (2002), p. 68.

of expenditure on clothes, food and daily necessities has fallen by a large margin, while expenditure on housing, telecommunications, medical and health care, education and recreation has risen rapidly. In 1999, the consumption expenditure of urban and rural households on the latter categories accounted for 29.3 per cent and 21.6 per cent of total expenditure respectively, or an increase of 8.2 per cent and 6.2 per cent over the figures for 1995. In 2000, the Engel coefficient for urban households (the proportion of food expenditure in total consumption expenditure) was about 40 per cent, or a drop of almost 10 per cent from that in 1995 and 18 per cent from that in 1978. Meanwhile the Engel coefficient for rural households was about 50 per cent, or a decrease of about 8 per cent from that in 1995 and approximately 19 per cent from that in 1954[14] (Table 2.6)

While taking measures to improve people's living standards across the board, the Chinese government has attached great importance to ensuring that poverty-stricken people have enough food and

Table 2.6   Changes in the Engel coefficient, China, 1954–2000 (per cent)*

	1954	1978	1995	2000
Urban households	–	58	50	40
Rural households	69	–	58	50

* The proportion of food expenditure in total consumption expenditure.

clothing. Since the initiation of reforms and the opening up of China in 1979, the government has conducted a large-scale, development-oriented aid-the-poor drive across the country in a planned and organised way. It has helped more than 221.8 million rural people to be adequately fed and clothed and has reduced the number living in poverty from 250 million in 1978 to 28.2 million in 2002.[15] According to the United Nations, China's achievements in this field provide a model for other developing countries, and even for the whole world. At present, over 95 per cent of rural people in China have enough to eat and wear, and about 25 per cent of rural Chinese live well-off lives.[16]

The huge improvements in living standards have greatly improved people's health. On average, life expectancy rose from 35 in 1949 to 72 in 2002, or 10 years longer than in developing countries and about the same as in moderately developed countries.[17]

With the rapid economic and social development of the country, China's sporting achievements have also improved. At the Olympic Games in 2000, Chinese athletes won 28 gold medals, 16 silver medals and 15 bronze medals, ranking China third in the world. In major international games in the past five years Chinese athletes have won 485 world championships and broken 193 world records.[18] All these universally acknowledged achievements illustrate the flourishing of the Chinese nation at the turn of the century.

International responses to China's rejuvenation

Observers of and researchers on China throughout the world have paid tribute to its development efforts, which have resulted in 'rejuvenation and national rebirth'[19] after nearly two centuries of stagnation and backwardness. In the words of Immanuel Hsü, an eminent American historian, 'Like a phoenix rising from the ashes, China enters the 21st century in the best international position it has known since the end of the Ch'ien-lung period (1735–1795).'[20]

As early as 1998, three former American presidents and 24 former high-ranking officials wrote to the US Congress to point out that 'China will become a great economic and political power in the 21st century', and suggested that suitable adjustments should be made to meet the new situation.[21] One expert even predicted that 'it may well be that when the history of the late 20th century is written 100 years from now, the most significant event will be the revolutionary change in China, which will soon be Communist only in a rhetorical sense.... For more than a century, the United States has been the world's largest economy. The only nation with a chance of surpassing it in the next generation...is China.'[22] With regard to the date when China's GDP will surpass that of the United States, experts predict that it will take place between 2006 and 2015 (Table 2.7). According to Hsü, China's 'century-old search for wealth, power, and international respect seems to be within reach. China's growing economic, military and political clout has earned it international recognition as a regional superpower in Asia-Pacific, and an emergent world superpower possibly by 2020.'[23] Moreover, it is expected that China will 'play a major role in world politics. The United States, which can no longer single-handedly play the role of "the policeman of the world", needs China to be a stabilising force in Asia and has accorded it a "strategic partnership"'.[24]

It is generally thought that by the middle of the twenty-first century China will have completed its modernisation and one fifth of the

Table 2.7 GDP growth, China, the United States and Japan, 1994–2015 (PPP, 1994 values billion dollars)

	1994	2000	2006	2010	2015	*Average annual growth rates (%)*
United States	6704	7791	8852	9 657	10 673	3.0
Japan	2593	3114	3642	4 277	4 509	4.1
China[1]	4950	6602	8808	10 665	13 569	4.9
China[2]	2989	5096	8087	11 002	15 431	8.1
China[3]	2695	4160	6600	9 000	12 600	7.6
Percentage of GDP US:						–
Japan	38.7	40.0	41.1	44.3	42.2	–
China[1]	73.9	84.7	99.5	110.4	127.1	–
China[2]	44.6	65.4	91.4	113.9	144.6	–
China[3]	40.2	53.4	74.6	93.2	118.1	–

Notes:
1. Estimates by the Rand Corporation.
2. Calculated according to 1994 purchasing power parity by the World Bank (1996).
3. Calculated according to the 1994 value of per capita GDP (PPP).
Source: Hu and Wang (1998), p. 46.

world's population will have entered modern society. Hu Angang, a leading expert on contemporary China, sees this as 'the most important achievement in the development history of human beings. Its significance is equal to the great achievements of human society since the industrial revolution ... Also, it is of more far-reaching significance than the rise of the United States in the second half of the nineteenth century, and the rise of Japan and Asia's "Four Small Dragons" after World War Two.'[25]

As discussed earlier, China was a closed economy until 1979. Its rapid economic growth from then onwards was the result of its opening-up and reform strategies, which transformed its relationships with the rest of the world and accelerated its modernisation drive. Importantly, the reforms were accompanied by a deepening of global integration, which served to broaden and intensify China's international linkages in trade, investment and finance. In other words, China's national rejuvenation has kept pace with economic globalisation and contributed much to world economic development. Furthermore, China possesses the biggest potential market in the world for consumer goods and capital investment, as well as offering a large pool of low-cost labour, which are all important for advancing global economy.

According to the World Bank, China will account for some 40 per cent of the increase in developing country imports between 1992 and 2020, thus helping to drive growth in world trade. Moreover, industrial countries will benefit from China's growing demand for imports of capital- and knowledge-intensive manufactures and services, and the primary products as well as from gains in the terms of trade. Neighbouring developing countries are also likely to experience significant gains.[26]

China's rise to the status of economic superpower will change the world's economic, trade and investment structure. According to Hu and Wang (1998, pp. 25–6), because China's GDP and export growth rates are so high they will contribute greatly to world GDP and the global export market. In addition, its success in solving its development problems in terms of population control, employment, grain production and so on provides an example for the rest of the developing world to follow. Finally, as a member of the United Nations it will be an important force in maintaining peace and security in Asia and the rest of the world.

China's national rejuvenation is one of the most important events of human society at the end of the twentieth century and the outset of the new millennium. The history of the world will take note of this splendid change, making China a stronger and more prosperous country contributing still more to the cause of human progress, as the marvel of our era.

3
The Part Played by Chinese People in Bringing About Reforms

When examining China's rapid economic growth and social development over last two decades, credit must be paid to the crucial part played by the Chinese people. With great courage and wisdom, those people concerned with the China's destiny and future never stopped in their observation and consideration of China's situation, and tried their best, often at great risk to themselves, to offer criticisms and suggestions. It was their valuable efforts that finally enabled China to launch the reform and opening up drive by the end of 1978. In exploring the associated events we shall consider three groups of people – intellectuals, officers and common people – each of which used different methods to give impetus to and played different roles in China's development.

Intellectuals as pioneers in pushing forward social change

After the founding of the People's Republic of China a large number of intellectuals with foresight and sagacity, dared to voice their opinions on and criticisms of the handling of state affairs. Their unswerving efforts gradually led to new patterns of policy making and state administration. The economist Ma Yinchu (1882–1982) ranked high among these critics.

Ma Yinchu and his 'New Population Theory'
Ma Yinchu, also known as Yuanshan, was born in Shengxian (now Shengzhou) in Zhejiang province. He studied economics in the United

States and was awarded a doctoral degree, thus becoming the first doctor of economics in China. After returning to China, he first worked as a professor in the Department of Economics at Beijing University and subsequently became chairman of the department and dean of the university. After the founding of the People's Republic, he held many important posts, including vice chairman of the North China Military and Administrative Commission, vice chairman of the Financial Commission of the Government Administration Council, president of Zhejiang University and president of Beijing University, as well as being a member of the Chinese Academy of Science.

In 1953, he began to look at the question of population control and conducted investigations in ten or more counties in Zhejiang province. After three years of research, in 1955 he wrote a paper entitled 'Population Control and Scientific Research'. Two years later, on 2 March 1957, he presented his ideas to the participants at the Supreme State Conference. He argued that while a large population was a significant resource it also imposed a heavy burden on the country in terms of economic development and living standards. His proposed solution was to control the size of the population by means of family planning. However, his 'new population theory' was severely criticised and he was unfairly treated for a long time[1] because his idea was contrary to that of Mao Zedong, who argued that the bigger the population, the better the economic reconstruction. Despite this, Ma stuck unwaveringly to his theory and when Zhou Enlai, then premier of China, suggested that he make a self-criticism he refused to do so.[2] On 25 December 1959, he published a declaration that 'Although I am almost eighty years old, and I am fully aware that the few cannot withstand the many, I will certainly meet the attack single-handed and never draw back. I will never surrender to those who coerce people by force instead of convincing them by reasoning.'[3]

After many years, eventually Ma's proposal was accepted and he was made honorary president of Beijing University, a member of the Standing Committee of the National People's Congress and a member of the National People's Political Consultative Conference. Ma was the first to raise the issue of family planning and his perseverance exemplified the strong sense of accountability among Chinese intellectuals and the important role they played in state affairs.

By now, the rapid growth of the population had become a very serious concern. In the 15 years between the founding of the People's

Republic and 1964, the population increased from 500 million to 700 million; that is, it took an average of 7.5 years for the population to increase by 100 million. Between 1964 and 1974, the population rose to 900 million, or an average increase of 100 million over five years. From 1973, family planning was promoted throughout the country and the time needed for the population to increase by 100 million was lengthened to about seven years.[4]

By 1999, the birth and natural growth rates had fallen to 15.23 per cent and 8.77 per cent respectively, compared with 33.43 per cent and 25.83 per cent in 1970. The total fertility rate of Chinese women dropped below the replacement level, giving China one of the lowest fertility rates in the world. Over 300 million births were averted, resulting in great savings on the upbringing of children, relaxation of the pressure on natural resources and the environment, accelerated economic development and improved living standards.[5] Despite the magnitude of this achievement, if Ma's proposal had been adopted when he put it forward in the mid-1950s, some 2–300 million more births would have been averted.

Sun Yefang and the law of value

Another outstanding intellectual who stood firm in voicing his ideas to help the government adjust its economic policies was the economist Sun Yefang. Sun had studied in Moscow and had joined the Communist Party in 1923 when he was just 15. In the mid-1950s, Sun started to study socialist economic theory while working as director of the Institute of Economics Studies at the Chinese Academy of Science. For a long time before the reform, economists in China were keen advocates of China's traditional socialist economic system. Their ideas were based on the principles of Marxist economics and they drew on Marx's works when conducting their theoretical research. However, a small number of economists, including Sun, were critical of the traditional system and offered proposals for reform. At the heart of Sun's proposal was the achievement of maximum effectiveness at minimum cost. He called for the economic plan to be put in the context of the law of value, based on his understanding of Marxist economics and with reference to the contradictions of the economic system. Some of his critiques did occasionally influence decision making, but he was severely criticised for his advocacy of the law of value, the use of a profit indicator in economic management and the giving of some degree of autonomy to enterprises. It was believed that these ideas ran counter to socialist theory and would damage the integrity of China's economic system.[6] In the early 1960s, Sun was condemned as 'the number one revisionist of the economics circle in China'. He came under incessant criticism and was denounced by all sides. In April 1968, he was imprisoned for seven years. During his time in prison he was refused access to pen and paper but he still managed to continue his work on economic theory. He rethought and mentally revised his 22-chapter book *On Socialist Economy* no fewer than 85 times! In his mind, 'Death is not too high a price for my work. It also doesn't matter if my reputation is damaged. However, the theories and ideas of economics obtained from my long-term research cannot be given up. I must live for the truth. I must leave my ideas with other people before my death so that they can make a just judgement.'[7]

After the Cultural Revolution, he expressed his view that the ten years of turmoil had served to reverse the desirable condition of maximum effectiveness at minimum cost and resulted in minimum achievement at maximum cost. In the subsequent years, Sun's ideas were gradually accepted and most of his proposals for reform of the economic system have now been put into practice.

Gu Zhun and the socialist market economy

Gu Zhun was indisputably one of China's most profound thinkers and shrewd observers. He was a senior revolutionary, he had joined the Communist Party in 1935 when he was 20. In 1949, when Shanghai, the largest city in China, set up a new government he was appointed as first director of the Shanghai Bureau of Finance and Tax. Like many young Chinese people in the first half of the twentieth century, his motives for joining the party and becoming a part of the revolutionary force were to destroy the autocratic institutions that had dominated China for thousands of years and to found a new China based on democracy and science.

After the founding of the People's Republic, Gu witnessed several serious incidents that stemmed from dogmatism and arbitrary decision making. He eventually took an uncompromising stand against such practices and accordingly was made to suffer by upholders of the ideas and policies that dominated at the time. However, he never stopped theorising and never stopped opposing those whom he considered to be in violation of the truth. In 1957, he published an article entitled 'On Commodity Production and the Law of Value under the Socialist System', thus becoming the first scholar to raise the important idea of a Chinese socialist market economy. In his view, development should follow the market mechanism in accordance with China's actual circumstances. He stressed that it was essential to adjust production in line with fluctuations in market prices so as to deploy resources effectively. This idea showed considerable foresight and remains important and practicable today.[8] He was twice branded as a rightist, which was a very rare occurrence for China's 55 million rightists. In order to live a normal life and avoid trouble and danger, his wife divorced him and his five children renounced their relationship with him. Nevertheless, he persisted with his ideas.

Gu Zhun's legacy to the Chinese people consists not only of his works but also his outstanding spirit, character and independent way of thinking. More than 20 years after his death, his research is at last being made public. Today, his ideas are still seen as pioneering and fresh. Sun Yefang, who was discussed earlier, once declared that Gu had influenced his decision to put forward his theory on the law of value in the 1950s.

Hu Fuming and his advocacy of 'practice as the sole criterion for testing the truth'

On 11 May 1978, the *Guangming Daily*, the most important newspaper in China's academic circles, published an important article entitled 'Practice is the Sole Criterion for Testing the Truth' by Hu Fuming under the *nom de plume* 'Special Commentator'. At the time of the Cultural Revolution, Hu was a young lecturer in the Department of Philosophy at Nanjing University. Soon after the outbreak of the Cultural Revolution, Hu was accused of being a member of a reactionary gang for the president of the university. He was criticised, denounced, paraded through the streets and subjected to public insult. His personal experiences caused him to condemn the countless injustices that had occurred during the Cultural Revolution, and to explore the nature of and reasons for this so-called revolution. The main ideas expressed in the resulting article were: (1) social practice should be the sole criterion for testing the truth; (2) the unification of theory and practice was a basic principle of Marxism; (3) those revolutionary mentors, such as Marx and Lenin, are the models of adhering to testing truth by practice; and (4) all theory should be tested continuously in practice.

Hu emphasised that it was vital to understand and study new things, but we cannot use the existing formulas to restrain, castrate and tailor the colourful revolutionary practices that are rapidly developing.[9] This historic article prompted a nationwide discussion on the criteria for truth that had far-reaching repercussions.

People began to break free of the bondage of leftist ideology that had dominated China for so long, emancipate themselves from the spiritual shackles of doctrinairism and the cult of personality, and readopt the Marxist principle of 'seeking truth from facts'. It also played a part in the struggle against the Gang of Four and setting things to right in every field of endeavour, as well as forming the ideological basis for the convening of the Third Plenary Session of the Eleventh Central Committee of the CPC.[10] In short, Hu Fuming's article ignited the fuse of ideological emancipation throughout China.

Before writing his powerful article, Hu had been neither a well-known scholar nor a person of academic or political note. His actions illustrate the bravery, insight and sense of social responsibility of Chinese intellectuals of that generation, whose spirit and sense of morality have since given impetus to the process of social development.

The part played by officers in political and institutional change

Fan Zhongyan, a famous politician in the Northern Song dynasty, said that a good politician should 'be the first to worry about the affairs of the state and the last to pursue personal enjoyment', a dictum that he followed all his life and was perpetuated by public-spirited people over the centuries, including many officers of the newly constituted People's Republic. During the first 30 years of the republic, such officers put considerable effort into formulating ideas for adjustments to state institutions and policies that would benefit China's development and people's lives. Foremost among these brave soldiers were Peng Dehuan and his supporters, and Zhang Zhixin.

The Voices of Peng Dehuai and his supporters

Marshal Peng Dehuai was a legend among the generals of the Chinese People's Liberation Army. In 1954, Peng became minister of defence and a member of the Politburo, and in 1955 he was made a field marshal of the Chinese People's Liberation Army. In July 1959, the Politburo held a conference at Lushan Mountain in Jiangxi province, to discuss a number of economic problems caused by the Great Leap Forward.

The Great Leap Forward, the People's Commune Movement and the 'General Line of Socialist Construction' were known as 'The Three Red Flags' of China's economic reconstruction, the aim of which was accelerating economy development so as 'to catch up with and surpass the United Kingdom within seven years and...the United States within fifteen years'.[11] The Great Leap Forward mainly involved labour-intensive industrialisation, typified by the construction of thousands of small steel furnaces to increase iron and steel production, and the launching of so-called 'satellites of high yields' – a trend or tendency then to boast and exaggarate one's achivements in farming production in order to meet the requirement of the wrong policies. The People's Commune Movement blindly chased the poorly planned communisation of agriculture.

The Three Red Flags movement, which swept over China within a very short time, had catastrophic consequences. The national economy was thrown into disarray, causing huge economic losses and mass starvation. Peng could not keep silent about this awful situation and wanted to express his views and suggestions on correcting the leftist line. Peng would have preferred to talk with Mao in person, but when he went to Mao's residence in the afternoon of 12 July the latter was sleeping. Peng therefore decided to write a letter.[12] He pointed out various problems associated with the Great Leap Forward and suggested that the key reason for these problems was 'petty-bourgeois fever'. After he submitted his letter a number of other high-ranking leaders who were attending the conference – including Zhang Wentian (an alternate member – a candidate for a formal vacancy or a preparatory member – of the Politburo and First Deputy Foreign Minister), Huang Kecheng (Deputy Defence Minister, Deputy Secretary-General of the Military Commission of the Central Committee and Chief of the General Staff of the People's Liberation Army) and Zhou Xiaozhou (First Secretary of the Party Committee of Hunan Province) – delivered speeches on similar concerns to those felt by Peng, and called for the mistakes of the Great Leap Forward to be redressed.

In a three-hour speech, Zhang Wentian systematically analysed the severe problems that had been caused by the Great Leap Forward. With regard to the reasons for the mistakes, 'we cannot stop at the explanation of lack of experience, but need to explore our way of thinking and working style'. He argued that if the role of the subjective initiative of man were to be stressed excessively, it would become subjective idealism. Therefore, to guide economic development China 'must not rely only on political commands ... but must follow objective economic law'.[13] Zhang called for a democratic party style and the cultivation of an environment that would allow subordinate party members to express their opinions. 'Why can't we listen to opposing opinions? Listening to opposing opinions is an important component of adhering to the mass line and seeking truth from fact.'[14] This amounted to a veiled criticism of Mao's style.

In their speeches, Huang and Zhou supported Peng's views and criticised leftist mistakes, which greatly irritated Mao. Huang considered that Peng's speech had some shortcomings and that the existing problems could have been emphasised more strongly. In respect of the emergence of unrealistically high targets for agricultural yields, Zhou pointed out that this was due to subordinates wishing to exceed the goals set by the higher authorities.[15]

The original reasons for convening the Lushan meeting had been to review the experiences of economic construction and the lessons learnt since the launching of the Great Leap Forward in 1958, and to redress leftist mistakes. However, due to Peng's letter and the speeches of his supporters the orientation of the meeting rapidly swung from redressing leftist mistakes towards anti-rightism. Mao considered that Peng's letter revealed the 'vacillation of the petty bourgeoisie' and constituted 'an antiparty programme of rightist opportunism'. Hence, the conference wrongly launched a criticism of Peng and his followers.[16] Critics of Mao's line were labelled antiparty and were deprived of their governmental and party posts. Later, this criticism resulted in a nationwide anti-rightist movement, which weakened party political life and strengthened the leftist mistakes of the Great Leap Forward. Moreover, it escalated the theory and practice of class struggle, which culminated in the Cultural Revolution seven years later.

The actions of Peng and the other dissenters show that some high-ranking officers were bold enough to voice their convictions, despite the risks involved.

The courage of Zhang Zhixin

Zhang Zhixin was a young female officer of the propaganda department of the party committee in Liaoning province. Although Zhang was only a junior officer, she took great interest in state affairs and the direction of change. Careless of her own safety, after the start of the Cultural Revolution she publicly criticised the evil actions of Lin Biao, (Vice-Chairman of the Central Committee) and the Gang of Four. She claimed that they were deliberately creating unprecedented havoc and disaster while plotting to seize power. She also criticised Mao. She stressed that Mao should be credited with many great achievements in the past, especially during the democratic revolutionary period before 1949, but pointed out that he had made mistakes during the years of socialist revolution and economic construction. These included the launching of the Great Leap Forward regardless of the objective realities, which had resulted in three years of great difficulty in the early 1960s, and the launching of the Cultural Revolution, which had exacerbated the leftist mistakes made within the party since 1958. Moreover, these mistakes had spread outside the party, with severe consequences for every area of the economy. Zhang was particularly critical of the personality cult that prevailed at the time, and argued that no one should place themselves above the party.[17]

All the issues raised by Zhang were sensitive and discussion of them was forbidden, so it came as little surprise when she was arrested and charged with being an 'active counterrevolutionary', which at the time was the most feared accusation in China. Despite being tortured severely while in prison, she remained true to her convictions. After seven years' imprisonment she was sentenced to death and was executed on 4 April 1975. Today, it is unimaginable that people who expressed ideas that did not accord with those of the authorities would be dubbed an enemy of the revolution and the country, and might even be killed. Zhang Zhixin understood this danger but was willing to risk her life to fight wrong doings by the state. She was a real hero of contemporary China. Four years later she was exonerated, and the solemn story of her great spirit stirred the nation.

What was the reason for such extreme treatment during the Cultural Revolution? Was it simply because it was a time in which black was confounded with white and right was confounded with wrong?

As pointed out by Ren Zhongyi, former party secretary of the provinces of Heilongjiang, Liaoning and Guangdong and a former member of the Central Committee:[18]

> A people's democratic dictatorship means a system in which the great majority of the people enjoy democracy but dictatorship is applied against a small minority of enemy forces. But in the past only the dictatorship part...was actually implemented....Lin Biao and the Gang of Four applied dictatorship to everybody and...in the realms of culture and thought as well. They interpreted dictatorship as the right to oppress. They made people shut up. And whoever was dissatisfied became an intellectual dissident, an enemy of the revolution and might even be killed. The Liaoning martyr Zhang Zhixin is a classic example of this. They ruined the families and destroyed the lives of tens of millions of people. And they called it a paradise. They brought the country to the edge of collapse. At the third session of the Eleventh Congress the Party corrected the error that 'The Class Struggle is the Most Important Thing'. The Party made a firm distinction between contradictions with the enemy and contradictions among the people.

This section has explored attempts by Chinese officers, ranging from an ordinary official to a marshal, to promote the country's development by criticising misguided state actions and policies without consideration for their own safety. The story of Gu Zhun, which was discussed earlier, should also be included in this category as he was a local government officer. Their great bravery is representative of that of the many thousands of officers who contributed to the building of a more democratic, more modern society with rule by law.

The part played by ordinary people in bringing about change

There is an ancient Chinese maxim that every individual is responsible for the prosperity or decline of his or her country. The people who gave impetus to the reform of Chinese society were not only intellectuals and officers but also ordinary people with foresight and courage.

Yu Luoke, a young human rights thinker

Yu Luoke was a young and an heroic thinker. When heredity, which can be compared to the caste system in India, escalated in China with the launching of the Cultural Revolution, Yu condemned the practice in a long thesis entitled *On Parentage*.

According to heredity, 'dragon bears dragon and phoenix bears phoenix, the son of a mouse is able to burrow', therefore 'the son will be a fine fellow if his father is a hero, and the son will be despicable if his father is a reactionary'. Thus, millions were deprived of the rights enjoyed by others simply because their fathers or grandfathers were landlords, rich farmers, counterrevolutionaries, rightists, 'bad elements' or 'capitalist roaders', in short anybody who did not belong to the revolutionary classes. They did not have the right to join the army, enter higher education and obtain employment. This type of discrimination emerged in the late 1950s and gathered momentum during the Cultural Revolution. As can be imaged, it inevitably caused many social problems including sharp social conflicts and instability.

Yu Luoke had a good high school record in terms of both character and scholarship. However, he was twice refused the right to sit the university entrance examination because his parents had studied in Japan and had run a privately owned ironworks after their return to China. In other words, his parents were deemed to be capitalists. In order to understand this social phenomenon, Yu studied the social science classics, ranging from Marx to Rousseau.

In the early stages of the Cultural Revolution the Red Guards responded to Mao's declaration that 'to rebel is reasonable' and went on a rampage against so-called feudalism, capitalism and revisionism. They feverishly promoted hereditary accession and shouted derogatory slogans at the top of their voices. In the process, many people were severely maltreated. It was during this time that Yu published *On Parentage*, which fiercely condemned heredity. Yu's ideas received strong support from millions of people but incurred the wrath of those in power. He was arrested as a counterrevolutionary in early 1968 and two years later, having refused to renounce his ideas, he was executed. In a bitter twist of fate, soon after his death the policy towards heredity was changed and people from non-revolutionary family backgrounds were treated as 'subjects who could be educated'.

Wang Shenyou's challenge to the Cultural Revolution

Wang Shenyou was a young working-class student with an independent mind. He aspired to be a scientist in order to serve his country and entered the physics department of Eastern China Normal University in 1963 when he was only 17. He studied very hard but found the time to concern himself with political affairs both at home and abroad. When he started his higher education, leftist thinking was prevalent. In line with this, the university cancelled the study of foreign languages and reduced the time allocated to academic study in order to make way for political study and work practice in factories and the countryside. Wang was opposed to these measures as they would negatively affect students' academic study. He recorded his thoughts in his diary, the contents of which were leaked to the authorities and as a consequences he was subjected to criticism.

In June 1966, at the beginning of the Cultural Revolution, he saw the dangers inherent in this political movement and was determined to resist it. His sympathies lay more and more with the so-called 'reactionary academic authorities' and 'capitalist roaders'. He wrote in his diary that the convulsions caused by the Cultural Revolution would set back the country for at least ten years.

Wang was branded a reactionary, his home was ransacked and all his diaries – dating from middle school to university – were exhibited as evidence of his opposition to socialism. Later he was put into prison, where he taught himself German – he had already learned Russian and English. Upon his release, he was sent to labour at the May 7th cadre school, a farm whose purpose was to remould cadres during the Cultural Revolution. During his time there, Wang read the original works of Marx and Engels, which fundamentally changed his worldview. Under very difficult circumstances, he began to analyse China from the viewpoint of dialectical and historical materialism. He used every opportunity to collect economics material that would aid his research.

After returning to university from the cadre school Wang was put under constant surveillance. One day he refused to show his surveillant a letter he had written to his girlfriend. The letter was seized and he was thrown into jail again for writing reactionary material. In prison he was asked to reword the contents of his letter. Instead, and in just six days, Wang wrote a 60-thousand word statement in which he detailed his political ideas and views. This came to be called Wang's 'confession'.

The statement covered his thoughts on the Marxist worldview, the history of the Soviet Union, the history of China, the Cultural Revolution and Chairman Mao. He condemned the anti-rightist movement and the Cultural Revolution. He paid credit to Mao's great achievements before 1949 in guiding the revolution and founding the new China, but criticised Mao's mistakes after 1949, saying that the Great Leap Forward and the People's Commune Movement showed elements of utopian socialism. He poured scorn on the Gang of Four. He expressed concern about China's poverty and backwardness, and stated that this could be remedied by the development of a commodity economy and foreign trade. China's closure to the outside could not continue. As could be expected, his statement was ill-received by the authorities. In the spring of 1977, he was sentenced to death and he was executed in April.[19]

Wang Shenyou's analysis and suggestions were later evident in the policies and practices adopted after the Third Plenary Session of the Eleventh Central Committee of the CPC, convened in December 1978. Thus, his theoretical research, single-minded pursuit of the truth and far-sightedness eventually made an invaluable contribution to the progress and development of Chinese society.

The part played by collective action

The driving forces behind China's political and social development consisted not only of courageous individuals but also mass movements, including the April 5th movement and the Xiaogang village household contract responsibility system.

The April 5th movement

The April 5th movement, which began to take shape in early 1976, was a nationwide mass protest against the damaging deeds of the Gang of Four. In 1975, Deng Xiaoping, with the support of Mao Zedong, had taken charge of the day-to-day work of the Central Committee of the party and State Council, and had begun to consolidate work in all fields, bringing about a marked turn for the better in the domestic situation. However, Mao, as the organiser and leader of the Cultural Revolution, could not accept Deng's systematic correction of the mistakes of this movement, which he saw as one of the two most important things he had done in his life (the other is overthrowing the regime of the Kuomintang and founding the People's Republic). Hence, by means of propaganda and animadversion compaigns he did all he could to undermine Deng's influence.

In January 1976, Premier Zhou Enlai passed away. People throughout the nation mourned the death of this much-loved leader in different ways and began to express their discontent with the Cultural Revolution. However, the Gang of Four, in their bid to usurp the power of the party and the state, were bent on stifling all mourning. On 9 January, two days after Zhou's death, Yao Wenyuan of the Gang of Four told Lu Ying – his trusted follower and general editor of the *People's Daily*, the number one official newspaper – to play down the death of the premier: foreign countries' telegrams of condolence should be given little space, the newspaper should not advocate the wearing of mourning bands and the sending of wreaths, and the words 'respected and beloved premier Zhou Enlai' should not be used.[20] On 5 March, the *Wenhui Bao*,[21] an important newspaper controlled by the Gang of Four, cut out Premier Zhou Enlai's inscription to Lei Feng, an eminent moral model in China since 1949, from an article published in that day's newspaper. And then, on 25 March, the Gang of Four stated that 'The capitalist roader in the party had wanted to help to power the capitalist roader who had been knocked down but still refused to repent.'[22] Quite clearly the first 'capitalist roader' was Zhou Enlai and the second Deng Xiaoping. The wicked words and deeds of the Gang of Four stirred up great indignation and people's long-suppressed emotions erupted like a volcano.

As the Qing Ming Festival – the traditional Chinese day of remembering the dead – approached, the popular uprising against the Gang of Four began to take shape. What came to be called the April 5th movement started in Nanjing, where Zhou Enlai had fought zealously for the communists in the 1940s. On 28 March, more than 400 students of mathematics at Nanjing University went to the new village of Plum Garden, a place of historical importance to Zhou, to mourn his death. Thereafter, thousands upon thousands of people from factories, government departments and universities followed suit and Plum Garden and the Yuhuatai Martyrs' Monument were submerged in wreaths.

On 29 March, about 300 students from Nanjing University took to the streets to put up protest posters. In Nanjing railway station, with the support of the staff, they painted slogans on railway carriages, including 'Down with those who opposed Premier Zhou!', 'Be vigilant against persons like Nikita Khrushchev assuming power!' and 'Uncovering the evil backstage supporters of the *Wenhui Bao*!' These slogans were read and adopted throughout the country as the trains travelled to and fro. On 31 March, a slogan proclaiming 'Down with the careerist and machinator Zhang Chunqiao!'[23] appeared on a large mansion and received a warm welcome from the public. The Gang of Four were galvanised into action, and using all the legal power they usurped, to scotch the movement. They even libelled the action of Nanjing people 'opposing the Party Centre' and 'trying to split the CPC centre'.

While this call resulted in cruel suppression,[24] the Nanjing people refused to bend. Moreover, it stirred up great rage in other parts of the country and protesters began to converge on Beijing and eventually triggered off the April 5 movement. From morning till night on 3 April, about a million people flocked to Tiananmen Square to lay wreaths and poems in honour of Zhou Enlai and condemn the Gang of Four. While the term 'Gang of Four' was not used directly, it was clear that 'demons and ghosts', 'jackals', 'White Bone Demon', 'machinator' and 'careerist' referred to them. On April 4, the day of the Qing Ming Festival, the activities in Beijing reached their climax. Up to two million people flooded to Tiananmen Square and added to the mountain of wreaths and poems. That night, prompted by Gang of Four member Jiang Qing and others, the Politburo convened a meeting considering the actions 'instigated by the counterrevolutionaries to oppose the party centre and Chairman Mao, and to... jeopardise the main direction of the class struggle'.[25] It was decided to remove the wreaths and forbid the continuation of mourning.

Five thousand militia, 3000 policemen and 200 lorries were immediately dispatched to Tiananmen Square to clear it of all wreaths, poems, scrolls and slogans. In the morning, a huge crowd of shocked and angry people gathered in the square in protest. When the authorities refused to return the wreaths, the crowd pushed over and set fire to the car of the deputy commander-general of the Beijing Workers' Militia and burned down the headquarters of the Militia, Police and Garrison Command, which was located on the south-east corner of the square.

The Politburo and Mao labelled the protest a counterrevolutionary incident. Deng, who was deemed to have been embroiled in the event, was dismissed from all his posts, both inside and outside the party. At 9.30 that night, Tiananmen Square was besieged by 10 000 militia, 3000 policemen and five battalions of PLA troops, who brutally assaulted the protesting masses and made countless arrests.[26] This repression of the April 5th Movement caused even greater unrest and heralded the end of the Gang of Four. Four weeks after Mao's death on 9 September 1976, all four were put under arrest.

The April 5th Movement had a significance beyond its immediate aims in that it brought about the rehabilitation of Deng Xiaoping and to a great extent established the political foundation of reform coming soon. In December 1978, the Central Committee of CPC decided to cancel its campaign of criticism against Deng and reverse the official judgement of the Tiananmen incident.

The Xiaogang village household contract system

For a long time, influenced by leftist thinking, the authorities in China linked the nature of ownership to the nature and stability of the regime, and thought that the larger the size of a production operation and the greater degree of the state ownership, the greater the progress of economic construction, especially in the countryside. However, the 'big in size and collective in nature' model failed in practice because it was not able to encourage farmers to do more and better; on the contrary, it greatly dampened the enthusiasm of the peasantry and caused numerous problems.

The iron rule that 'ownership consists of three levels, with the production team as its foundation'[27] was inviolable and it was politically dangerous to question or challenge it. Farmers were only allowed to work on collective land in a collective way, and those who tried to grow vegetables around their houses or keep a few pigs in order to earn money to buy rice or other grain were condemned as taking the capitalist road and ordered to stop. The human cost of this policy was huge. For instance, in 1978 in Fengyang, the county in which Xiaogang village was located, the number of people who fled from famine and went begging rose to 23000, and the population of the county fell from 0.468 million to 0.378 million. Within a few years in Xiaogang village alone, 60 people starved to death and 76 had to leave the village to seek a living elsewhere.[28]

In this situation, farmers had little choice but to find another model of production. In December 1978, Yan Hongchang, deputy head of the production team in Xiaogang village, assembled the members of the 18 households that comprised the team and proposed that the collective land be divided and a portion allotted to each household for contract farming, a practice that was strictly forbidden. The aim to do so was to link remuneration to output, in contrast to the prevailing practice of paying all farmers the same amount, regardless of performance. Yan proposed that each household should sign and stamp a contract to produce sufficient grain to pay the annual grain tax, and never to ask for money and food from the state. If any of the cadres were imprisoned or killed as a result of their actions, other members of the team would bring up their children until they reached the age of 18.[29] With some trepidation, the 18 households subsequently put their name, stamp or thumbprint on the contract drawn up by Yan. Thereafter, the eagerness of the farmers to improve production grew markedly and, by the end of the second year, their combined grain yield had increased from 15000 kilograms to more than 60000 kilograms. For the first time ever Xiaogang village was able to pay its grain tax to the state and repay its loans.

This brave venture by the Xiaogang villagers was the first trickle of a deluge of reforms to Chinese agriculture. When knowledge of it first emerged, the shockwaves travelled from the local administrative level to the centre. Fortunately, by then the nationwide discussion about the criteria of the truth had been conducted and won the decisive victory, and the third plenary session of the Eleventh Central Committee of CPC, which had determined to launch overall reforms, had convened. The Xiaogang village's creativity soon gained acceptance. The system received the firm support of Wan Li (the former Vice Premier and Secretary of the Party Committee of Anhui province then, who had been condemned during the Cultural Revolution as a capitalist roader) and Deng Xiaoping, who had just been rehabilitated. The system was approved by the Central Committee in January 1982 and promoted throughout the country. By the end of 1982, 78.7 per cent of the production teams in rural China had adopted the system. In 1983, the figure rose to 93 per cent, and in 1985, the last 249 of the 12000 or so people's communes broke up. With them went the system of state monopoly on the purchase and marketing of agricultural and sideline products, which had lasted for more than 30 years.[30]

Li Rui and his proposal for reform of the political system

With the start of the twenty-first century, China entered a new era. After 24 years of successful reform and rapid social and economic development, China reached the stage where the political system was acting as a bottleneck to further development. However, reform of the power structure, the operating mechanisms of the government, the relations between party and the government and the supervision and balance of state power were highly sensitive issues. Although the existence of these issues has been widely known, it is still crucial to make systematic and concrete analysis and to set forth the goal and the way to deal with these problems. Many scholars and officers with far-sighted views devoted themselves to this research. Among them, one who must be particularly noted is Li Rui, a former secretary of Mao Zedong and a holder of high office. Due to his status as an intellectual, a high-ranking senior officer and a veteran of the communist revolution, his views were especially influential.

At the sixteenth National Congress of the CPC in December 2002, Li delivered a speech entitled 'A Proposal about China's Political System Reform', which was the result of protracted deliberations, numerous consultations and many amendments. Li's proposal covered ten points: five on democratisation of the party system and five on a move towards constitutional government.

With great concern for China's destiny and future, he pointed out that to ensure social stability, catch up with the times and global practices, and improve economic development, it was necessary to reform the political system and speed up the introduction of democratic politics. He particularly emphasised the fact that the history of both China and foreign countries had shown that autarchy was the fundamental cause of social upheaval.[31] The following were his key recommendations.

First, it was necessary to abolish life-long tenure for leading cadres. Moreover, the situation that the leading cadres flowed in turn from the party positions to the government, and then to NPC and finally to CPPCC, due to their aging, should be ended as soon as possible. Second, leading cadres should be selected on the basis of multicandidate elections at the National Congress, including the members and standing members of the Politburo and the general secretary.

Third, as the National Congress was the highest authority, the Central Committee should only exercise power in periods when the Congress was not in session. Moreover, in order to be effective, Congress deputies should have permanent tenure. With regard to effective intraparty supervision, the Commission for Inspecting Discipline at each level and the Party Committee at the same level must be parallel bodies – both of which should be elected by and accountable to the Party Congress at that level – and should work in tandem, rather than maintaining the present system of the former working under the leadership of the latter.

Fourth, to ensure optimum decision making there should be full freedom of expression within the party. All members should be free to voice their opinions on key issues, both at party meetings and in the press, and should have the right to criticise any member of the party, including the top leader. All crucial issues should be decided subject to collective discussion and put to the vote, rather than being determined by the first-in-command. Finally, the party should operate in full accordance with the constitution and no individual or organisation should have the right to step outside the constitution. In the then current situation, the party outweighed the law and rule by man outweighed rule by law.[32]

As noted above, Li also made five important suggestions about the democratisation of political life of the state. He pointed out that there had long been a constitution but no constitutional government. According to the constitution, the National People's Congress was the highest authority, and therefore it should not be led and commanded directly in the name of the party. It was the responsibility of the party to adhere to, enforce and safeguard the constitution. It was essential to set up a Constitutional Court and to enact laws to protect people's interests and rights, and to enable people to supervise the running of the party and the government.[33]

Li's proposals stirred up considerable interest in both academic and political circles. Indeed, in December 2000, when Hu Jingtao, the new general secretary of the CPC Central Committee, held the first study of the Politburo, the main topic was the constitution. Some commenters considered that this signalled the coming of constitutional government.[34] In any event, it showed that Li's proposals had made an impression on China's leaders.

This chapter has considered various pressures for reform by Chinese people with a strong sense of social responsibility and insight, including intellectuals, cadres and common people. Their stories are typical of those of many people who opposed what had proven now to be wrong ideologies and wrong guidelines for the running of China. Their main targets were as follows:

- Personality cults and ideological control
- Highly Central-planned and mandatory economy system
- The Cultural Revolution and its disastrous effect on the people
- The lack of freedom of expression over state affairs
- The absence of choice over lifestyle
- Social inequality.

There can be no doubt that their criticisms and suggestions gave great impetus to the changes that were made to the traditional institutions, ideologies and policy-making models, and eventually resulted in the radical reforms and the start of national rejuvenation. As in the past, the people will continue to generate the fundamental dynamics of the further development of Chinese society.

Today's China is a very different place from that of two and a half decades ago. The cult of personality has all but disappeared and the people no longer need to call out 'long live' anyone. There is no longer a requirement to put pictures of the top leaders in public places. A democratic climate is gradually emerging: people have more freedom of expression and can criticise policies, institutions and even the leader without worrying about their safety, as long as they do not take direct action against the government or the state. Central planning of the economy has been replaced by one operated with a market-oriented mechanism. The Chinese people now have the freedom to set up their own businesses and protect their property. There are fewer restrictions on foreign travel for the purpose of study, trade, investment and tourism. Last but not least, people have more opportunity to participate in the running of state affairs. To a large extent these historic changes can be credited to the efforts of people such as those discussed in this chapter.

4
The Part Played by Chinese Leaders Since 1978

A crucial factor in China's national rejuvenation was the capable leadership provided by top politicians since 1978. China's new leaders were adept at observing and balancing complex situations both at home and abroad and, unlike previous leaders, they resolutely concentrated on China's economic reconstruction and social development with a sense of historic mission. The four key reasons for the success of this group are discussed in turn in the following sections.

The selection of Deng Xiaoping as paramount leader

When discussing the role of leadership in the reform and opening up of China to the outside world, it is first necessary to discuss the events leading up to the rehabilitation of Deng Xiaoping.

For any leading group in a country, choosing a suitable and competent leader-in-chief is vital if the desired goals are to be realised. Because of China's power structure, operating mechanisms and political elitist tradition, this choice was even more important. China is still a country in which a paramount leader with great authority is not only to be accepted and requested by the society, but must also be able to play a very important role. In early October 1976, the smashing of the Gang of Four ended the catastrophic Cultural Revolution and provided the possibility for China to enter a new era. At that time, Hua Guofeng,

Mao's chosen successor, was the Chairman of the CPC Central Committee and Premier of the State Council, which actually controlled the power with his followers. However, fundamentally speaking, Hua was not one who could be competent at his duty. That Hua was selected by Mao as successor and took up his positions stemmed from a very special situation. In early 1976, Mao's health had been steadily deteriorating and choosing a successor had become a very urgent task. Mao had realised that Jiang Qing[1] and the other members of the Gang of Four would never be supported by the people, but the alternative group of high-ranking possibilities, headed by Deng, had been opposed to the Cultural Revolution, which Mao saw as one of his major lifetime achievements. In contrast, Hua Guofeng had loyally implemented Mao's policies during the Cultural Revolution and could be trusted to continue them.[2]

After the downfall of the Gang of Four, Hua faced four difficult issues: (1) his legitimacy as Mao's successor, (2) the rehabilitation of Deng Xiaoping, (3) evaluation of the April 5th movement and the Cultural Revolution, and (4) re-establishment of the economic order and its future modernisation. Having a vested interest in the Cultural Revolution and its leftist thinking and policies, it was impossible for Hua to evaluate it objectively. Indeed, what Hua said and did since he took up position as the Chairman of the Central Committee and of its Military Commission, indicated that he was not completely politically competent to assume such a crucial position. For instance, he set forth his erroneous idea of 'two whatevers', namely, 'upholding whatever policy decisions Chairman Mao made', and 'unswervingly adhering to whatever instructions Chairman Mao gave', in January 1977.[3] Actually, 'two whatevers' became Hua's weapon to oppose the rehabilitation of Deng and denying the Cultural Revolution. What is more, in his political report delivered at the Eleventh National Congress of CPC convened in August 1977, Hua still strongly emphasised the following very wrong ideas: adherence to 'the theory of continuous revolution under the proletariat dictatorship', insistence that 'the Cultural Revolution is absolutely necessary' and should continue along strict leftist lines, and he declared that economic reconstruction should be governed by politics and conducted as a mass movement in the style of the Great Leap Forward.[4] Thus, Hua and his followers intended to perpetuate theories and policies set forth by Mao from the late 1950s, especially those of Cultural Revolution.

As discussed in the previous chapter, the Cultural Revolution was a catastrophe – '20 million people died, 100 million were made to suffer, and 800 billion Chinese yuan were wasted'.[5] Thus, if China was to develop, it was imperative to get rid of all vestiges of the Cultural Revolution, including ultra-left thinking and also to prevent conservative forces from controlling the central power. According to the party constitution, the party chairperson should be elected, not appointed, but Hua's position came from the former way and he worried about this. Since Hua and his followers had vested interests in the Cultural Revolution, they wished to keep the established power structure with Hua as the core. He did not want others to challenge his power and did not allow denying the Cultural Revolution by which their positions were obtained. However, by implication of the group supporting Deng, Hua realised that his 'assumption of the chairmanship of the Central Committee and of its Military Commission could be deemed unconstitutional; but if he would agree to the reinstatement of Deng, this question of legitimacy could be negotiated or even withdrawn. Thus, the two issues came to balance. As a result of mediation by Marshal Ye and Vice-Premier Li Xiannian, who desperately desired a smooth transition to the post-Mao era, Hua agreed in principle to rehabilitate Deng, and to revise the five-year economic plan to accelerate the four modernisations.'[6] In late November 1976, Hua announced that Deng's reinstatement would be discussed at the Central Committee meeting in July 1977. In return, he received the support of Ye, Li and others for his continuation as Chairman of the Central Committee.[7]

The reinstatement of Deng was an important milestone in post-Mao China as it brought about the possibility of strengthening the more healthy forces in the CPC central authority. With Deng at the core, the strength of the reform-oriented group grew, while the authority of the conservative group headed by Hua Guofeng and Wang Dongxing gradually declined and they were eventually ousted. From then onwards, Deng and his supporters went all out to set right past wrongs. History has proved that to select and support Deng as the paramount leader of the core authority of the central power in post-Mao China was a decisive step for China's leading group targeted at reform, proving it to be a powerful authority with cohesiveness, creativity and efficiency.

The redressing of past social and political wrongs

As soon as they had stabilised their power and the domestic situation, China's post-Mao leadership, headed by Deng, proceeded to resolve the difficult issues left over from the previous era and to readjust China's political and social relations according to their reform-oriented thinking and strategies. This was considered essential to mobilising the people behind China's modernisation.

The task of redressing the wrongs done to people who had been unjustly or falsely accused and sentenced – which had been started two years earlier after the downfall of the Gang of Four but had progressed only slowly – now began in earnest. These people included early leaders of the party and the state, leaders of various ethnic groups or communities, cadres at all levels, advocates of democracy, intellectuals, workers and peasants. Between 1979 and 1982, the central and local authorities addressed numerous major cases, including those of Peng Zhen (a former member of the Politburo and Mayor of Beijing), Lu Dingyi (a former alternate member of the Politburo, Vice-Premier of the State Council and Minister of Culture), Luo Ruiqing (former Vice-Premier of the State Council, Chief Secretary of the Military Commission of the Central Committee and Chief of the General Staff of the People's Liberation Army), Xi Zhongxun (former Vice-Premier of the State Council and Chief Secretary of the State Council), Chen Pixian (former Secretary of the East China Bureau of the Central Committee and First Secretary of the Party Committee of Shanghai) and Ma Yunchu (former President of Beijing University and Vice-Chairman of the Economy and Finance Commission of the central government). Later, the Central Committee issued a series of notices declaring that all those who had been wrongly labelled as rightist opportunists because they had reported practical realities or expressed opinions that differed from those of the party should be exonerated, as would all those who had been wrongly criticised in newspapers or official documents of the central and local authorities and military department. These matters would be redressed, and all the vilifications and falsehoods would be cancelled completely. Thus Zhang Zhixin, Shi Yunfeng and the countless others who had been persecuted for opposing the groups headed by Lin Biao[8] and Jiang Qing[9] in the Cultural Revolution were exonerated, and all those who had been unjustly accused of wrong doing were rehabilitated.[10]

One of the severest cases of injustice was that of former president Liu Shaoqi, who had been stripped of all his positions during the Cultural Revolution and had been harassed to death in prison. In February 1980, the Central Committee of the CCP resolved to redress Liu's case by withdrawing the labels imposed on him (including 'traitor' and 'agent provocateur') and to counteract the Central Committee's resolution of October 1968 'to expel him from the Party forever and to dismiss him from all the posts in or out of the Party'.[11] (At that time, some 71 per cent of the original members and alternate members of the Central Committee had been labelled 'traitors', 'spies' and 'anti-party elements').[12] Moreover, Liu was rehabilitated as 'a great Marxist and proletariat revolutionist, a chief leader of the party and the nation', and on 17 March 1980, the Central Committee held a memorial ceremony for him. Along with Liu, more than 28 000 people who had been wrongly judged as anti-revolutionist for being implicated in Liu's case were exonerated.[13]

After a series of hard efforts, by the end of 1982, the work of redressing the cases in which people were unjustly, falsely or wrongly charged or sentenced, carrying out all over the country on a large scale was basically completed. These mishandled cases involving 3 million cadres have been redressed. More than 470 000 CPC members have been reconverted, and millions upon millions of cadres and the masses involved in the various mishandled cases have extricated themselves from misery. Including the cases of those who had been wrongly labelled 'rightist', nearly 553 000 of the latter[14] were politically rehabilitated and awarded better employment and salary arrangements.

The second measure was to revise the class status of landlords and kulaks (rich peasants). On 1 January 1979, the Central Committee resolved that those landlords and kulaks who had abided by the law and laboured well for years should henceforth be classified as commune members. Their issues should be subject to no discrimination in terms of education, recruitment to the army, membership of the Chinese Communist Youth League, membership of the Communist Party, employment assignment and so on. More than four million such people were reclassified.

The third group to be addressed consisted of former members of the Kuomintang, the nationalist political party that had dominated China before the founding of the PRC. On 1 January 1979, the Central Committee agreed that all former members of KMT who had rebelled or surrendered to the communists should be forgive for their past misdeeds, awarded equal rights, given work suited to their abilities and resettled properly. As a result of this policy, more than 400 000 former members of the KMT received new treatment. In addition, in March 1982, the Standing Committee of the National People's Congress decided to review the cases of imprisoned members of the Kuomintang party, government and army, plus former Kuomintang secret agents. By June that year, more than 7000 prisoners and 55 000 compulsory labourers in reform units had been released and given political rights.[15]

The fourth measure was to readjust the ethnic minority policy so as to promote national unity. In March 1979 in Lhasa,[16] 376 of those who had participated in the Tibetan Rebellion of 1959 were released from prison and more than 6000 were relieved of their label as rebels. In April in the Ganzi and Ahba prefectures (autonomous areas inhabited by people of the Zang nationality in Sichuan province), 588 prisoners who had participated in armed rebellions before 1960 were released and 363 former prisoners had their label of 'rebel' removed. Throughout China, all who had been labelled as nationalists because they had sided with the right wing from 1957 were relieved of their labels, and all who had been wrongly labelled were exonerated.[17] These moves greatly improved overall social stability in China.

The fifth measure was to introduce a policy on religion, as this too would help maintain societal harmony. In July 1980, the State Council announced that the property rights to religious groups' houses would be returned to the original owners, or in cases where this was impossible, compensation would be paid. In addition, churches and temples that had been appropriated during the Cultural Revolution could be returned to their original use. Thereafter Buddhist, Taoist and Christian organisations throughout China began to resume their activities. In March 1982, the Central Committee circulated a 'Notice on China's Views and Policy on Religious Issues in the Socialist Period'. This document analysed the leftist policy on religion in the past and set out the basic requirements for readjusting and implementing a correct policy or religion.

Reform of other policy areas included the intellectual policy and the policy of affairs concerning nationals residing abroad and compatriots in or from Taiwan and their relatives. These and the measures detailed above show that the post-Mao leaders were genuinely reform-oriented and willing to correct past mistakes. This not only served to win them the trust of the people, but also reduced social conflict and laid a solid political foundation for the normalisation of national political life. History has proved that their efforts provided the necessary conditions for uniting the people behind China's development in a new epoch.

The unswerving adherence to the central task of economic construction

For much of the first 30 years of the People's Republic, class struggle and command politics were the guiding principles behind state policies and programmes. With the rise of the Cultural Revolution, continuous revolution under the dictatorship of the proletariat came to the fore. Eventually, the more leftist an idea or programme was, the more revolutionary and acceptable it was thought to be. Under this situation, to directly emphasize and advance the economic construction became a dangerous tendency. On the contrary, making politics a focus and criteria in dealing with and judging everything in every field of state life was becoming more and more popular, for doing so had a greater sense of political security for the people. Needless to say, the chaos of the Cultural Revolution had catastrophic consequences for the Chinese economy.

Soon after the end of the Cultural Revolution, the new leaders began to concentrate on reducing the gap between China and developed countries and newly rising rapidly developing countries as soon as possible. This would require a shift of focus by the party and the state towards economic construction and the goal of building China into a modern socialist economy by the end of the twentieth century.[18]

When talking about the bitter consequences of neglecting economic construction, Deng Xiaoping, the chief architect of the subsequent reforms, pointed out that:

Having experienced many twists and turns in our work during the past 30 years, we have never really been able to shift its focus to socialist construction. Consequently, the superiority of socialism has not been displayed fully, the productive forces have not developed in a rapid, steady, balanced way, and the people's standard of living has not improved much. The decade of the 'cultural revolution' brought catastrophe upon us and caused profound suffering. Except in the event of a massive war, we must steel ourselves to carry out this task with constancy and devotion; we must make it our central task and allow nothing to interfere with its fulfillment. Even if there is a large-scale war, afterwards we will either pick up where we left off or start over. The whole Party and people should form this high resolve and keep to it without faltering.[19]

He went on to say:

Since our modernization programme covers many fields, it calls for an overall balance and we cannot stress one to the neglect of the others. But when all is said and done, economic development is the pivot. Any deviation from this pivotal task endangers our material base. All other tasks must revolve around the pivot and must absolutely not interfere with or upset it. In the 20-odd years since 1957 we have learned bitter lessons in this respect.[20]

The dedication of China's leaders to economic development soon became evident in practice, and over the years numerous important programmes were carried out. They remained true to their goals despite a series of political disagreements and social upheavals, including the pro-democracy demonstrations in 1986 (for which party chief Hu Yaobang was dismissed from his post in 1987)[21] and the mass demonstrations that culminated in the turmoil in Tiananmen Square in June 1989. Zhao Zhiyang, Hu's successor, was ousted from office for his handling of the latter demonstrations.[22]

More recently, when the SARS epidemic was in full swing, Premier Wen Jiabao pointed out that while China was still experiencing rapid economic growth and improved returns, some sectors had been hit by the SARS outbreak and therefore extra would be required for the rest of the year to make up for the losses.[23] This illustrates the point that, no matter what circumstances arose, successive leaders of post-Mao China remained unswervingly dedicated to sustained economic development.

The unswerving pursuit of reforms and opening up

As is well known, China's remarkable economic growth and social development over the recent past is the result of radical reforms and the opening up of the economy to the outside world. From the end of the 1970s, the aim of the reforms was the step-by-step development of a socialist market economy. In the traditional planned economy, commodity and financial markets and private ownership were forbidden. Hence, the establishment of a market-driven economy based on socialist principles had epoch-making and revolutionary significance.[24]

This was not a project that could be completed in a short time. Rather, it had to be accomplished in stages, starting with improvement of the existing system. The first sector to be tackled was agriculture. The household contract system (see Chapter 3) was gradually phased in and peasants became producers with the right to manage their own production. This meant that centrally planned agricultural production was done away with and a system of contractual purchases was introduced. The prices of the main agricultural products purchased by the state, such as grain and cotton, were increased substantially, and permission was given for markets for other agricultural products to be set up in rural and urban areas alike. Meanwhile, in cities, experiments were conducted on increasing the autonomy of enterprises and reducing central planning of production and sales. These efforts were preliminary steps towards the establishment of a market-driven economic system.

Four years later, in 1982, the reform experiences in urban and rural areas were reviewed and it was decided to divide the central plan into a mandatory plan and a guiding plan. The relevant government departments were asked to use the law of value, prices, taxes and credit as economic levers to persuade enterprises to meet the aims of the plans. Obviously, the authorities' understanding of the market was still quite limited, but a significant step away from traditional economic thinking had been taken.

With the deepening of rural reform and large gains in agricultural productivity, the focus shifted from country to city. In 1984, the Central Committee confirmed that, based on public ownership, development of a commodity economy was a necessary part of social and economic development and essential to China's modernisation. In March 1993, following the deepening of reform practices, 'the state practices socialist market economy' was enshrined in the constitution. Moreover, on 14 November it was decided that market mechanisms should be given full play in respect of resource distribution to ensure the optimum allocation and use of resources.[25]

The official establishment of a socialist market economy was an historic moment that reflected the leaders' unceasing dedication to the reform process. Although there had been disagreements about commodity–monetary relations, the necessity of applying the law of value and the role of the market in economic activities, these had been overcome and no longer obstructed the drive for economic development. From then on, growth accelerated. Between 1993 and 1996, GDP grew at an average annual rate of 11.6 per cent, the highest since 1949.[26] Moreover, inflation fell from 21.7 per cent in 1994 to just 6.1 per cent in 1996.[27] This was an outstanding performance that few transition or developing countries could match.

The development of China's socialist market economy included reform in many key areas, including the ownership system, the structure of the rural economy, the enterprise system, the price system, the administrative system, income distribution and foreign trade and investment.

Reform of the ownership structure

While state and collective ownership continued to dominate, some private ownership was gradually permitted in all economic sectors. In the past, the political ideal of 'ownership by all the people' had not only obstructed individual initiatives but also caused problems for state-owned and collectively owned enterprises as the absence of competition had dampened the enthusiasm needed to develop an effective productive force. However, during the 1980s, in order to address employment problems in urban areas and occupy surplus labourers in rural areas, the government had progressively encouraged the development of collective and individual ventures. As can be seen in Tables 4.1 and 4.2, private enterprises grew rapidly and made

Table 4.1 The share of state-owned, collectively owned and privately owned enterprises in GDP, 1978–96 (per cent)

	State-owned	*Collectively owned*	*Privately owned*
1978	56.0	43.0	1.0
1993	42.9	44.8	12.3
1996	40.8	35.2	24.0

Source: Zhang (1998), p. 18.

Table 4.2 The share of state-owned, collectively owned and privately owned industrial enterprises in gross output, 1978–97 (100 million yuan)

	State-owned	*Collectively owned*	*Privately owned*	*Other*
1978	3 289	948	–	–
1990	13 064	8 523	1 290	1 047
1995	31 220	33 623	11 821	15 231
1997	29 028	43 347	20 376	20 982

Source: Zhao (1999), p. 53.

an increasingly larger contribution to the national economy and economic growth. This new pattern of ownership was conducive not only to economic development but also to promotion of the market mechanism and intersectoral competition.

Another breakthrough in reform of the ownership structure was separating public ownership and the form of public ownership, thus solving the theoretical problem of combining public ownership with market economics. In practice, actually, at different stages of economy development different forms can be adopted for one type of ownership, and one form can be adopted for different types of ownership. In other words, the form of ownership does not directly determine the nature of ownership. Thus, it was decided at the Fifteenth National Congress of CPC that the form of public ownership should be diversified and all managerial methods and organisational forms that conformed to the law of socialist production should be encouraged. It was essential to find forms of public ownership that would facilitate the development of productive forces. For instance, the Western share system was effective in separating ownership from management, to the benefit operational efficiency. If capitalism could use a share system in such a way, so could socialism.[28] Separating public ownership and its format further removed the trammels that traditional thinking had imposed on economic development.

Reform of the rural economy

As noted earlier, China's reform effort started in the countryside. The reform programme consisted of four stages. First, the people's communes were phased out and replaced by the household contract system, which combined joint management with independent production. Second, through reform of the distribution system, a market system for farming and agricultural products emerged. Third, a break from the traditional pattern of rural development paved the way for rural industrialisation and urbanisation. Finally, measures were put in place to promote agricultural modernisation and rural industrialisation.

As a result of these measures, the rural economy took the lead in China's development. The new economic arrangements and liberalised policies fired peasants' enthusiasm and led to an unprecedented rise in productivity and agricultural yields (Table 4.3). Meanwhile, the burgeoning township enterprises not only played an important part in changing the economic structure of the countryside but also contributed greatly to China's economic growth. By the late 1990s, rural industrial output accounted for one quarter of national GDP and 130 million surplus labourers had been absorbed by township enterprises.[29] With this booming of the rural economy, household incomes increased markedly and living standards rose (Table 4.4).

Table 4.3   Agricultural yields, major crops, 1978–99 (10 000 tons)

	1978	1985	1990	1995	1997	1999
Grain	30477	37977	44624	46661	49417	50800
Oil-seed crops	522	1578	1613	2250	2157	2600
Cotton	217	415	451	477	460	–

Sources: Zhao (1999), pp. 40–1;
China Statistical Bureau (2000), http://www.stats.gov.cn.

Table 4.4 Per capita income, rural households, 1980–2002 (yuan)

	1980	1988	1992	1996	1999	2002
Gross income	151.79	990.38	2337.87	2999.20	n.a	n.a
Net income	133.57	686.31	1577.74	2090.13	2210.0	2476.0

Sources: Zhao (1999), p. 260;
China Statistical Bureau (2000, 2003) http://www.stats.gov.cn.

Reform of the enterprise system

In its efforts to reform enterprises in such a way that they would form the backbone of the socialist market economy, the government concentrated on four main tasks: (1) giving enterprises the status of legal entities, (2) reducing government's administrative jurisdiction over enterprises and to separate ownership from management, (3) building a modern enterprise system, and (4) revitalising the entire state-owned sector.

China's enterprise system had been set up to meet the requirements of the highly centralised economic system. Enterprises were given no autonomy and were unable to pursue their own economic interests. Instead, they were told what to produce and in what quantities. Furthermore, all decisions about personnel, finance and materials were made by the government authorities according to the central plan.

From the outset of the reforms, great efforts were made by the Chinese leadership to enable enterprises to become competitive corporate bodies. Reaching this goal required clearly defined property rights and management rights and responsibilities, separation of the functions of government from those of enterprises, and a scientific method of management. Experiments were conducted in the following areas:

- Transforming the management structure of enterprises
- Separating the right of ownership from the rights of management
- Introducing an internal improvement mechanism of modern enterprise
- Changing the factory system to a company system
- Changing asset operations to capital operations
- Introducing horizontal associations and management by groups of enterprises

- Setting up a contract responsibility system
- Creating new institutions and improving the external environment
- Restructuring and upgrading enterprises in accordance with adjustments to the national economic structure.

All these experiments contributed significantly to the eventual course of enterprise reform.

Reform of the price system

The architects of the reforms recognised that in a market economy both the means of production and the elements of production were commodities and each had its price. To encourage the formation of a market mechanism for prices, it was essential to reform the present system to include markets for capital, labour, production inputs and commodities. By 1997, the market was determining over 90 per cent of the prices of means of production and agricultural products, and over 95 per cent of the prices of industrial products. Moreover, statistics show that the prices of industrial products fluctuated in line with changes in supply and demand in the market.[30]

Reform of economic administration and control

Under the traditional system, the running of the national economy had been undertaken by a power-centralized system within a single administrative framework. There had been no distinction between the macroeconomy and the microeconomy, and therefore no system of macroeconomic control. To remedy this, the government gradually shifted from direct administrative management to indirect management. Then, a coordinated macroeconomic control system was set up and progressively refined.

The aim of this reform, as with all the other reforms, was to cater to the demands of a market operation. As pointed out by Jiang Zemin, General Secretary of the CPC, giving full play to market mechanisms and strengthening macroeconomic control were fundamental to a socialist market economy; neither was dispensable.[31] This implied that both an 'invisible hand' and a 'visible hand' were needed to advance the development of China's socialist market economy.

The reform of income distribution

The reform of income distribution was an important aspect of the reform effort. Before the reforms, leftist thought had been more concerned with preventing inequality than with people's lack of material goods. Egalitarianism was actually considered to be the fundamental aim of income distribution. Because extra work was not rewarded by extra pay, people had no incentive to work harder, which inevitably resulted in inefficiency and poverty. Since the launching of the reforms, the question of income distribution has been addressed by means of four measures. The first was to permit some people and some areas to increase their income through their own efforts. This would enable them to help others, and eventually wealth would trickle down to the whole of society. The second was giving priority to efficiency while ensuring fairness. Thirdly, came the principle that income distribution should not only consider one's performance at work, but also other elements involved in the production that one contributed, such as capital technology and so on. The fourth was to set up a multi-tier social security system.

Opening up to foreign trade and investment

The main contribution on the opening-up theory covered four aspects as follows. Abandoning the closed or half-closed development mode practised in the past and making opening-up a state's basic policy establishes an opening-oriented economy system and is the first contribution. Then, stressing the importance of absorbing all civilised achievements created in society, including those produced in capitalist society, and giving full use of the resources and markets both home and abroad is the second contribution. Furthermore, creating the theories of setting up Special Economic Zones and an outside-oriented economy system is the third contribution. Finally, confirmation that in promoting the opening-up course, the relationship between opening-up and regeneration through one's own efforts must be handled correctly is the fourth contribution.

With the guidance of these theories, China's leading group kept up efforts in pushing forward the development of China's opening-up. Thus China was able to absorb foreign capital, technology, information and managerial and intellectual skills. In 1992, China began to attract huge amounts of foreign investment (Table 4.5), and in 2002 it overtook the United States to become the world's top recipient of FDI. Opening up also enabled China to progress in the fields of science, technology, education and so on. Moreover, it is essential to take particular note that, as the 'windows, bridges and experimental fields' of opening-up to the outside world, China's Special Economic Zones played an important role in promoting this course. Overall, the implementation of the opening-up policy did much to advance China's modernisation and reduce the gap between China and the developed countries both economically and technologically.

Conclusion

Thanks to the unremitting efforts of China's leaders, fundamental changes have been made to China's economic system and operating

Table 4.5   Foreign investment in China, 1979–2002

	Number of investments	Contracted investment (billion US dollars)	Actual investment (billion US dollars)
1979–83	1 392	7.742	1.802
1984	1 856	2.651	1.258
1985	3 073	5.932	1.661
1986	1 498	2.834	1.874
1987	2 233	3.709	2.314
1988	5 945	5.297	3.194
1989	5 779	5.600	3.392
1990	7 273	6.596	3.487
1991	12 978	11.977	4.366
1992	48 764	58.124	11.007
1993	83 437	111.436	27.515
1994	47 549	82.680	33.767
1995	37 011	91.282	37.521
1996	24 556	73.276	41.726
1997	21 001	51.004	45.257
1998	19 799	52.102	45.463
1999	16 918	41.223	40.319
2000	22 347	62.380	40.715
2001	26 140	69.195	46.878
2002	34 171	82.768	52.743

Source: Zhang and Huang (2003), p. 79.

mechanisms. Central planning and control by administrative means over resources deployment have been abolished in most areas of economic activity, and the market mechanism is playing the main role in adjusting the production and distribution of commodities. The state has retained control over only nine types of agricultural product and 12 industrial products. The production of over 95 per cent of industrial products is now determined by the producers themselves according to swings in demand. Meanwhile, the overwhelming majority of commodity prices are governed by the market, which accounts for 92.5 per cent of retail sales of consumer goods. With regard to the means of production, market-adjusted prices account for 81.1 per cent of total sales. Finally, 79 per cent of the prices the state pays for farm products and sideline products are adjusted by the market.[32]

As well as the leaders' extraordinary achievements in the areas discussed in this chapter, they have also paid attention to the aspirations of the people and drawn on the wisdom of the masses, thus winning their sustained support for and enthusiastic participation in the country's development. Thus successive leaderships, headed from Deng to Jiang to Hu, have been able to devote themselves to building not only a strong economy but also a strong society in a rejuvenated China.

5
The Key Role of Deng Xiaoping

It is beyond doubt that Deng Xiaoping was the chief architect and promoter of China's reforms and opening up to the outside world. In other words, Deng was the crucial driving force behind China's modernisation and rejuvenation.

As Karl Marx pointed out, 'Every era needs its own great person. If there is no such person, it is necessary to make one.'[1] A great leader is one with foresight and sagacity who stands ahead of the tide and promotes development through guidance and/or astute policy making. Deng Xiaoping was undoubtedly such a person. He not only directed China's development but was also a key designer of the associated strategies and policies.

In China, Deng was considered an outstanding leader and he enjoyed high prestige throughout the country. He was praised as a great Marxist, proletarian revolutionary, statesman, military strategist, diplomat, reformist and founder of the theory of building socialism with Chinese characteristics.[2] Moreover, his extraordinary role in China's rejuvenation was widely acknowledged internationally. When he passed away on 19 February 1997, heads of states, governments and international organisations around the world praised his remarkable achievements. For example, Kofi Annan, Secretary-General of the United Nations, referred to him as 'a primary architect of China's modernisation and dramatic economic development.' He would 'be remembered, not just in his own country, which he so faithfully served for so long, but also in the international community at large'.[3] Similarly, President Boris Yeltsin of Russia spoke of him as having brought about historic changes in China,[4] British Prime Minister John

Major said that 'Deng's initiative played a crucial part in creating today's economically dynamic and successful China'.[5]

In emphasising Deng's role in promoting China's rejuvenation, it is essential to point out that it was his position as the paramount leader of post-Mao China that provided him with the power to direct and organise the historic change discussed in this book. China was a country in which people needed and believed in the concept of paramount political authority. Deng's status and power from the end of the 1970s was similar to that of Mao in the first 30 years of the People's Republic, but his prestige and influence came from the fact that his endeavours were aimed at benefiting the Chinese people and lifting the country out of poverty, while the reputation of Mao after 1949 was based mainly on an irrational personality cult that stemmed from his achievements during the communist revolution and the founding of the Republic. Ranking high among Deng's talents were his ability to prevent other top leaders from becoming embroiled in endless debates and controversies from which they would be unable to extricate themselves, and to counter criticisms of the necessity and conduct of the reforms and the opening-up process by leftist or rightist groups at various political levels.

Deng's main contributions to China's rejuvenation

As 'one of the most outstanding politicians of the twentieth century',[6] Deng Xiaoping was well versed in both civil and military affairs. He not only presided over a very long war as a chief military commander and made a remarkable contribution to the founding of the new regime, but later brought economic prosperity to the world's most populous country. His contributions to the rejuvenation of China covered the theoretical and the practical aspects.

Theoretical contributions

Ideological emancipation

Deng led three campaigns of ideological emancipation that were fundamental to the economic development of China. The first was aimed at breaking down the cult of personality and doctrinairism. Deng reintroduced the ideological line of 'seeking truth from fact' and pressed for abandonment of the 'two whatevers':[7] upholding whatever policy decisions Chairman Mao made and unswervingly adhering to whatever instructions Chairman Mao gave, which approach was supported by Hua Guofeng, then chairman of the CPC Central Committee. In Deng's view, if everyone just followed the book and thinking was allowed to remain rigid it would be impossible to forge ahead.[8] Only by adhering to the principle of 'practice is the sole criterion for testing the truth' would it be possible for China to correct past mistakes. The militaristic measures Mao had used to launch and conduct the Great Leap Forward and China's Soviet-style centralisation and mandatory planning were just such mistakes. This new line was diffused throughout the nation and set the stage for the subsequent reforms. The Chinese leaders were also thereafter expected to put their words into practice and demonstrate their competence by speeding up economic development, improving people's living standards and improving China's international status, according to their principle.

The second ideological emancipation was to break away from the idea that all aspects of the economy had to be centrally planned. In the late 1980s and early 1990s, China courted foreign investors, imported foreign techniques and adopted western managerial methods to further economic development, especially in the coastal areas. Some people doubted the wisdom of this and were concerned that it would change the nature of China's socialist enterprise, and eventually its socialist political system. However, Deng argued that having a planning-oriented or a market-oriented system was not the fundamental distinction between socialism and capitalism. The existence of a planned economy did not necessarily equate with socialism as capitalism also had planning, and the existence of a market economy did not necessarily equate with capitalism as socialism also had a market. Both were the means to an economic end.[9]

To address this sensitive issue, Deng set out three criteria by which to judge what would be deemed acceptable in China's economic construction. These later became known as the 'three whethers'. All proposed reform measures should be judged by whether they would be beneficial to the development of socialist productivity, whether they would strengthen the comprehensive power of the state, and whether they would improve people's living standards.[10] These criteria answered the main questions that had troubled people's minds and made it much easier to make decisions about the adoption of resources from Western countries.

Later, on Deng's instruction, the CPC Central Committee formally adopted a resolution that made the development of a market-driven economic system a lawful and urgent task. This in turn made it possible to deepen the reforms, accelerate the modernisation drive and further involve China in the global economy. The third ideological emancipation was to break away from the doctrine of full public ownership and to encourage the development of non-public or non-state ownership, including individual and collective ownership, foreign ownership and joint-venture ownership. While there was some concern that this would threaten state-owned enterprises, the backbone of the Chinese economy, application of Deng's 'three whethers' promoted acceptance of the coexistence of public and other sectors. The continuous economic growth since 1992 has proved the efficacy of the new ownership system, which 'not only facilitates economic development, but also promotes the formation of a vigorous and lively market mechanism whereby various economic sectors compete with each other'.[11]

Socialism with Chinese characteristics

Adherence to the socialist path was one of the four cardinal principles of the CPC, so China's economic development and the methods used had to conform to this principle. In 1982, Deng put forward the idea of constructing a socialism with Chinese characteristics and a modernisation programme that accorded with the Chinese reality, rather than continuing to rely on the lessons learned from the experiences of other communist countries.[12]

Deng's theory of a socialism with Chinese characteristics gradually took shape during the course of the reform process, based on the following propositions:

- The fundamental task of socialism was to emancipate and develop productivity to meet people's needs
- The development of the Chinese economy had to be adapted to China's reality as the country with the largest population in the world but a comparatively backward economy.

However, this meant moving into uncharted waters. There was no ready-made answer to be found in the classic Marxist works, and history had shown that Soviet-style economic construction, which had been copied by China for nearly 30 years, had failed and there were no successful cases to which China could turn for reference. Nevertheless, Deng's theory provided Chinese authorities with the direction needed for China's economic construction, together with unprecented flexibility.

Like Mao, who recognised that a successful communist revolution depended on the integration of Marxism with China's reality, Deng emphasised the need for a socialism with Chinese characteristics. Both Mao and Deng were successful in their endeavours, and 'history will take note of Mao's revolution and Deng's construction as two most powerful events in China – and to a degree in the world – during the second half of the 20th century'.[13]

China's relations with the outside world

China's one hundred years of humiliation at the hands of foreign powers and the possibility of further invasion in a new world war had strengthened its isolationist stance and hindered its development in the past. In the early 1980s, Deng, with great foresight, judged that the international situation would become one of détente between East and West, bridging the development gap between North and South. Accordingly, peace and development would be the two main themes of international relations, and this judgement has since been accepted by the world.[14] Based on this prediction, China turned its attention to economic construction rather than giving priority to preparing for a military response to world war. Two years after Deng's analysis, China cut the size of its armed forces in order to channel more money into economic development.

Having confirmed that peace and development are the main themes of the current world indicated that a very good international environment for economic construction was available for China. Hence, the degree of China's subsequent success owed much to its ability to seize promising opportunities when they arose.

Breaking down the egalitarian distribution system

As is well known, in the past China had a highly centralised and egalitarian distribution system, and those who tried to make extra money were seen as heading towards capitalism. This ossified thinking and strictly enforced system served to dampen the motivation and enthusiasm of the masses. Deng recognised the defects of egalitarianism and the need to increase people's motivation to improve productivity, and he suggested that this could be done by encouraging some people and certain areas to grow richer through honest labour ahead of others. Later, he pointed out 'that China's form of socialism was actually producing egalitarian poverty', and that what was needed was to smash the 'big rice-pot'[15] and egalitarianism.[16]

The theory and practice of allowing some people to improve their income ahead of others was significant not only in rural areas, where farmers could organise their own production, but also in urban areas, where workers in state enterprises, companies or authorities could be remunerated according to their performance or contribution in the form of innovative ideas, capital investment and so on. Such measures greatly motivated the masses and resulted in the flowering of the economy.

The reunification of lost territories: 'one country, two systems'

Bringing about the reunification of all Chinese territories was considered a key task in China's national rejuvenation – the loss of Hong Kong and Macau had happened when China was weak and invaded by Western powers, and the separation of Taiwan was a consequence of the civil war. It was deemed meaningless to talk about the national rejuvenation while Chinese land was still occupied by invaders or splintered from the motherland. Thus, it became urgent to bring about China's reunification. As Deng Xiaoping said in September 1982, 'if [Hong Kong] cannot be taken back in fifteen years the people will have no reason to trust us, and any Chinese government should leave power and quit the political scene'.[17]

Deng's theory of 'one country, two systems' was significant in promoting China's reunification. Because the social system in Hong Kong, Macau and Taiwan differed from that of mainland China, Deng's theory set out an institutional framework in which the two social systems could coexist in a united country and that respected the differences in political belief and way of life in the three regions. This theory received high praise from the international community. For instance, British Prime Minister Margaret Thatcher called it 'a creation of genius and a charmed idea', and said that it could 'open a new era ... [of] political philosophy'.[18]

Under the banner of 'one country, two systems', after a series of negotiations the Chinese government reached agreements with the

British and Portuguese governments, and Hong Kong and Macau peacefully returned to China in 1997 and 1999 respectively. The Taiwan issue is expected to be resolved eventually, thus bringing about the complete reunification of China.

Practical contributions

Deng's efforts in the mid-1970s

Deng's efforts to promote the modernisation of China began in 1973, when he was rehabilitated after being criticised, persecuted and stripped of all official posts at the start of the Cultural Revolution. In 1975, he was made Vice-Chairman of CPC Central Committee, Vice-Premier of the State Council and Vice-Chairman of the Central Military Commission and the General Staff of the Chinese People's Liberation Army, thus taking charge of the day-to-day affairs of the party, state and army. In order to remedy the catastrophic situation faced by China as a result of the Cultural Revolution and restore economic, social and political order, Deng put forward a comprehensive modernisation plan that reflected the aspirations of the Chinese people, who were weary of the upheaval of the past decades and the activities of the Gang of Four. With popular support throughout the country, Deng's version of the 'Four Modernisations' plan was carried out in a large number of sectors, ranging from railway transportation to the iron and steel industries, from education to scientific research and from defence to agriculture. Notable results were achieved in a very short time. In 1975 alone, the value of industrial output increased by 15.1 per cent and that of agriculture by 4.2 per cent.[19]

Unfortunately, Mao thought that Deng's actions amounted to a denial of the achievements of the Cultural Revolution, which Mao considered to be one of his major accomplishments. Consequently, Deng was again stripped of all his official posts. However, his efforts had formed a foundation for the crushing of the Gang of Four and the launch of reforms at the end of the 1970s. More significantly, his unswerving determination to push for China's economic development had won him the respect of the people, who demanded his rehabilitation after the smashing of the Gang of Four.

Economic reforms and opening up to the outside world

Deng was not only the chief architect of China's reforms and opening up but also their chief organiser and director. In 1997, Jiang Zemin,

General Secretary of the CPC Central Committee, placed Deng's accomplishments on a par with the revolution of 1911 and the founding of the People's Republic in 1949, the two most important events in modern Chinese history.[20] The revolution of 1911 had resulted in the overthrow of the Qing Dynasty and the end of feudal society; and the founding of the People's Republic had brought national independence and emancipation for the people. Deng's reforms paved the way for China to become a prosperous and powerful developed country, the dream of generations of Chinese people.

In September 1978, during an inspection tour of north-east China, Deng called on the people to 'accomplish the target of the Four Modernisations', which had first been mooted by Mao but obstructed by the launching of the Cultural Revolution. He stressed that 'We must accelerate the development of the productive force in line with [China's current] conditions, so as to enable people to live a better material...and...cultural life.'[21] Later the CPC Central Committee, in an historic turnaround, formally decided to abandon the guiding principle of 'taking class struggle as the key link' and to focus instead on economic construction. It was Deng who had pointed out that China's economic management was very inefficient and that if reforms were not carried out the modernisation drive would grind to a halt.[22] From then on his reform plans gradually took shape and he gave his support to all viable initiatives. For instance, he firmly supported the rural household contract system, which soon brought about growth in agricultural production, and the establishment of Special Economic Zones for foreign investors. These coastal SEZs developed with breathtaking speed and played a crucial part in China's opening-up process. Over the years, Deng was always on hand to provide direction for further development or answer questions. For example in 1992, at the age of 88, he undertook an inspection tour of southern China and answered a series of questions on the relationship between socialism and the market economy that had been perplexing people for a long time.

As mentioned earlier, it has been said Deng's reforms were as important as the revolution of 1911 and the founding of People's Republic in 1949. To understand this, it should first be remembered that the Chinese economy had experienced numerous difficulties and setbacks in the first 30 years of the People's Republic and was on the verge of collapse at the end of the Cultural Revolution. Second,

China had been very backward in terms of production. There had been insufficient arable land to produce enough food for China's huge population, the industrial infrastructure had been poor and resources had been in short supply. Although some economic progress had been made since the founding of the PRC, the productivity gap between China and developed countries had continued to widen. Third, the Soviet-style central planning system had prevented the development of efficient production. Finally, due to political hostility, military interference and economic blockades from outside and the leftist trend in Chinese foreign policy, China had been virtually closed to the outside world. This was one of the main reasons for the development gap between China and other countries.

Deng's reforms addressed all these problems, and in a comparatively short time the relaxation of central control, release of market forces and China's integration into the world economy boosted production to such an extent that China was lifted out of backwardness and poverty. (The great economic achievements during in this period are detailed in Chapter 2).

Ridding China of leftist thinking

There is a well-known saying in Chinese that past experience is a guide for the future. After the ten years of catastrophe of the Cultural Revolution, it was essential to reflect on these years and draw lessons for a future in which people's minds would be emancipated and they would be free to take initiatives. However, this was a very sensitive issue because most of the campaigns and policies that had caused the mayhem had been designed or permitted by Mao, based on his ultraleft ideology. Nonetheless, Deng faced up to the matter squarely and persuaded the party and the government to reflect on China's experiences prior to and during the cultural Revolution according to the principle of 'seeking truth from facts'.

In July 1981, a 'Resolution on Certain Questions in the History of Our Party since the Founding of the People's Republic of China' was adopted at the Sixth Plenary Session of the Tenth Party Congress. While praising past leaders' achievements since the founding of the People's Republic, which had laid the foundation for China's future development, the resolution pointed out three major mistakes that had been made during this period: the biased understanding of the political situation at home and abroad as a result of subjectivism, the excessive emphasis on class struggle, and aiming too high and advancing too hastily in the task of economic construction. These mistakes had inexorably led to the disastrous Cultural Revolution. Deng personally oversaw the drafting of this resolution, one of the purposes of which was to assess Mao's performance. In so doing, Deng's goal was to strike a balance between preserving the positive legacy of Mao's achievements prior to 1957 and criticising the negative ones thereafter, 'without jettisoning the Great Helmsman altogether as Khrushchev had done to Stalin'.[23]

Coming to clear conclusions about the rights and wrongs of past events was essential to prevent mistakes from happening again, to overturn wrong judgements of individuals and organisations, and to set up a political line that would loosen ideological control and unify the Chinese people in order to speed up the opening-up and modernisation process. With regard to past judgements, between the late 1970s and 1982, millions of people who had been unjustly imprisoned or labelled were exonerated, as discussed in detail in Chapter 4. This comprehensive redressing of past injustices won the hearts and minds of the entire nation and contributed significantly to social stability and economic development.

The three-step strategy for long-term development

Deng's three-step strategy for development between the early 1980s and the middle of the twenty-first century constituted the blueprint for China's rejuvenation. This followed on the heels of the Four Modernisations plan discussed above, which was aimed at raising China's GNP to $1 trillion and making the Chinese people 'comparatively well-off';[24] a concept that served to spur China's economic development from then onwards.

In April 1987, Deng presented his three-step strategy to the delegates at the Thirteenth National Congress of the CPC and it was later accepted by the party. The first target was to double GNP from its 1980 level and to meet people's basic requirements for food and clothing. The second was again to double GNP and bring people to the 'comparatively well-off' level. Finally, GNP would be brought to a level at which people would be relatively rich and modernisation would be fundamentally completed.[25] Deng's statement that although he would not live to see that day, he had a responsibility to set the target[26] showed his deep devotion to China's national rejuvenation.

Bringing about peaceful power transitions of core leadership

As an outstanding politician with great wisdom, courage and statecraft, Deng sucessfully promoted and completed two orderly power transitions, which have been proven as important factors for China's development in a peaceful environment.

The first leadership replacement took place during the early stage of the reform. After the smashing of the Gang of Four, a moderate group headed by Hua Guofeng (Chairman of the CPC Central Committee) controlled both the party and the state. Although Hua had rendered a great service by arresting the Gang of Four and was favoured by Mao as their successor, he was neither suitable nor competent to serve as chief leader. This had been proven by his actions from late 1976 to the end of 1978, before the convening of the third plenary session of the Eleventh Central Committee of CPC, which later became known as 'the period of indecision'. Politically, Hua supported the 'two whatevers' and refused to correct the mistakes of the Cultural Revolution and other leftist errors. Economically, he advocated a second 'great leap forward' and questioned the necessity of reforms and opening up. In order to lift China out of its economic and social difficulties, it was imperative to unseat Hua and his followers. With the support of other senior leaders who favoured reform, Deng progressively undermined Hua's authority ideologically, politically and organisationally, and in 1981, Hua and his followers were removed from office peacefully.

The second change occurred in the late 1980s and involved the group of reformers handing over the reins of power to a new generation. This move was of great significance because it marked the start of a retirement system for state leaders. For thousands of years, tenure in China had been life-long, especially in the case of people in high-ranking positions. This was extremely threatening to stability in that a chief leader might die unexpectedly early without having appointed a successor, thus leaving a power vacuum. Deng had long advocated the abolishment of this system and on several occasions had himself expressed a wish to retire. Realising that the retirement of advanced leaders could not be enforced at a particular time, Deng suggested that a Central Consultative Commission be set up as a transitional measure, and he took the post of chairman. In 1987, the 13th CPC National Congress agreed with his request to retire from the Politburo and the Central Consultative Commission. On 9 December 1989, he retired from his final post as Chairman of CPC Central Military Commission.

Deng created the conditions for and played a crucial role in the smooth transfer of power to a younger generation of leaders. This not only ensured the stability of the state and the sustained development of China's economy under the firm guidance of reformers, but also paved the road for orderly and peaceful transfers of power in the future.

How was Deng able to make such remarkable contributions to China's rejuvenation?

Unquestionably, it was not only the official status Deng possessed that enabled him to play such a great part in China's rejuvenation, but also his extraordinary qualities, capabilities and personality. Deng's military process as an army commander in the revolutionary wars and the war of resistance against the Japanese was well known, and the founding of the People's Republic offered him the chance to reveal his talents as a politician and statesman, especially after he went to Beijing and joined the central leadership. As a bright rising star, his performance soon attracted attention both at home and abroad.

Mao was one of the first to recognise Deng's political potential. During an argument in 1957 with Khrushchev, the General Secretary of the Soviet Communist Party, Mao pointed to Deng and warned the Soviet leader, 'Don't underestimate that little man, he destroyed an army of one million of Chiang's best troops.' He added, 'He has a bright future ahead of him.'[27] Much later, when presenting his recommendation for Deng's rehabilitation in March 1973, Mao paid a remarkable tribute:

Deng is a rare talent. He is known in both military and civilian circles for this. He is like a needle wrapped in cotton. He has ideas. He does not confront problems head-on. He can deal with difficult problems with responsibility. His mind is round and his actions are square.[28]

Before anything else, Deng was a great patriot. As he once told a Western correspondent, 'I am a son of the Chinese people. I love my motherland and people deeply.'[29] It was this strong feeling for his country and people that made him determined to build a powerful and modern China. Whenever the conditions were right, he did all he could to achieve this goal. When he was rehabilitated in 1977 he was 74, an age at which most people want to live an easy life with no hard work. Instead, as Chen later pointed out, This 'old man ... offered all his heart and remaining time to his own nation, and then paved a new epoch, and ... a brilliant road of ... national rejuvenation ... This may be the only case in history.'[30] During his time as paramount leader, he investigated every possible avenue to bring about the peaceful reunification of all Chinese territories, and expressed a wish to live long enough to stand for even a few minutes in Hong Kong when it was returned to China in 1997.[31] It was this strong patriotism that lay at the heart of Deng's fight for the development and rejuvenation of China.

Politically, Deng was good at judging situations and then making appropriate decisions; both were necessary qualities in a great politician. For instance, as discussed earlier, his prediction in the early 1980s that peace and development would become the main themes of international relations caused the central authorities to focus more on economic reconstruction and far less on preparing for the possible outbreak of a new world war. From the late 1980s to the early 1990s, there were numerous international disturbances. Deng's advice was to stand back and soberly observe what was going on, rather than involving China in the situation, and not to carry a banner (in dealing with the international affairs).[32] Under Deng's guidance, China thus safeguarded its independence, dignity, security and stability.

Another of Deng's attributes was that he always firmly adhered to his principles, including his political belief, his determined target, and his moral standard, even though this sometimes caused setbacks to his political career. For example, during the time of his first rehabilitation, Mao asked him to preside over a meeting of the Politburo in which the Cultural Revolution would be assessed as consisting of 70 per cent achievements and 30 per cent mistakes. To Mao's surprise Deng refused, saying 'it is not suitable for me to preside over this meeting. I live in the Land of Peach Blossoms without knowing the Han dynasty, or the dynasties of Wei and Jin.'[33] Deng never yielded an inch on this matter of principle, resulting in Mao again suspending all Deng's powers.

A similar example occurred before his second rehabilitation. After the downfall of the Gang of Four, pressure to restore Deng's posts was put on Hua Guofeng, Chairman of the Central Committee. Hua tried to block Deng's comeback, but when he realised that it could not be prevented, he tried to reach a compromise and requested that Deng write a statement that the April 5th Movement (see Chapter 3) had been anti-revolutionary. Despite this being a precondition for his return to office, Deng refused as he considered that the movement had been revolutionary in nature.[34]

While unswerving in his adherence to his principles, Deng was capable of great flexibility when dealing with concrete matters that would realise his desired targets. As he stressed in the early 1960s when encouraging peasants to be bold in finding ways to improve production, it did not matter whether a cat was black or white so long as it caught mice.[35] Some 20 years later, Deng applied the same idea to promoting the reform and opening-up course, which focused on the criteria of the 'three whethers' for judging the feasibility of adopting new policies or resources. The development of the Special Economic Zones and other reform measures were all the cases of applying this flexibility. By now the 'mice' in question were the continuing improvement of socialist production, of people's living standards and of state power.[36] All methods that could be used to catch these 'mice' were encouraged.

It is sure that Deng's combination of adhering firmly to principle and handling matters in practice with great flexibility was of key importance in enabling his success. Without adhering unswervingly to principle, he could not advance his desired cause with complete boldness and confidence; and without adopting great flexibility in coping with situations in practice, he could not efficiently and successfully push his strategy and approach towards his goal step by step.

Not least among Deng's attributes were confidence, an iron will and the ability to endure hardship. He always maintained his confidence when pursuing his targets, no matter how great the difficulties he encountered or how long it took. Deng was deposed three times during his political career, but each time he staged a comeback and each time he achieved greater success than before. Even Deng himself said that if there were a Nobel Prize for staging political comebacks, he would be very likely to be awarded one.[37] Deng attributed his ability to withstand so many setbacks to his talent for enduring hardship, which in turn depended on firm political conviction and exceptionally strong will.

Finally, in further exploration, more attributes of Deng could be seen to explain his success. He advocated and practised the principle of 'seeking truth from facts', always opposed empty talk and focused on down-to-earth hard work. He knew well his subordinates in order to assign them jobs that were commensurate with their abilities, and he was adept at selecting the right cadres to fill the most important posts. He was good at analysing historical experiences and learning from the experiences of other countries without copying them. He was good at mobilising the masses behind his strategies because he always showed respect to ordinary people and paid attention to their interests and aspirations. Compared with Mao, he paid far more attention to the economy than to ideological struggle and theoretical construction. Compared with Zhou, he had a stronger will, was more principled and was adept at making decisions at crucial moments. He won wide support all over the country, as well as great authority and prestige, which was a powerful resource in waging his unprecedented programme of national rejuvenation.

To sum up, Deng was the driving force of China's development in the post-Mao period. From the end of 1970s, he successfully stabilised and solidified the regime, and then organised and headed the reform and opening-up programme. His contributions to China's development were matchless and his contribution to overall world development can be seen as second to none in that China accounts for one fifth of the world's population. The American magazine *Success* selected him as the most successful man of 1985, in 1988 the newspaper *The World* depicted him as 'representing the spirit of the epoch' and the *Times Weekly* twice poured praise on him. It can only be assumed that the reason why other countries with civilisations and traditions as long as China's have not achieved the latter's remarkable successes is because they have lacked a leader with the characteristics of Deng.

6
The Fundamental Impetus Provided by the Chinese National Spirit

In exploring the dynamics of China's rejuvenation, one important element, the Chinese national spirit, should be given particular attention. Since the middle of the nineteenth century, Chinese people with lofty ideals have struggled for an independent, prosperous and strong modern country. This struggle has been driven by the Chinese national spirit, which is characterised by profound wisdom, solidarity and a great urge to become stronger.

The Chinese nation and its advanced civilisation contributed greatly to the world for thousands of years, but its development slowed from the mid-nineteenth century for various political, economic and social reasons. However, this situation was not likely to last. As Napoleon put it, China was 'a sleeping giant' and 'when he wakes he will move the world'.[1] Indeed, China began to forge ahead as soon the internal and external conditions were right. This chapter demonstrates that it was the powerful force of the Chinese national spirit that gave impetus to China's remarkable economic and social development from the late 1970s.

Looking back over the past five millennia, it is clear that without the driving force of the national spirit the Chinese nation would never have created its great civilisation, spread its influence to the rest of the world, united the numerous nationalities within its boundaries, fought against domestic and foreign oppressors, and won national independence and the people's liberation, and embarked on the voyage of national rejuvenation.

The Chinese nationalist spirit, which is the soul and backbone of the Chinese nation, blends traditional spirits with those of the present day: the spirits of self-improvement, humanity, diligence, exploration, creativity, moral integrity, patriotism, revolution, reform and opening up to the outside world.

The spirit of self-improvement

The spirit of self-improvement is the spirit of enterprise. Ancient Chinese philosophers said that a gentleman should never stop improving himself, and this can also be applied to the nation. Indeed, the history of China is a history of constant self-improvement. Constant self-improvement refers not only to struggle under normal or favourable conditions but also to struggle in times of adversity. Chinese elites and heroes over the centuries have cherished the idea of being a hero of men, or a 'gallant of ghosts', asserting that one can be poverty-stricken but one should always be iron-willed and never give up one's high aspirations. Moreover, in a life of poverty, one should pay attention to one's own moral uplift; in a life of power, one should help the people and society by managing state affairs.

Since ancient times, there have been countless examples of great achievements of writing under adversity. When Wen, the king of Zhou,[2] was imprisoned he took the opportunity to write the *Book of Changes*, or *I Ching*, a very important philosophical classic that explores how humans manage their relationship with the world and the interface between humans and knowledge which forms the basis of the Confucian and Taoist cultures. Confucius's life was full of misfortune but his *Spring and Autumn Annals* is one of the most important Confucian classics. Qu Yuan was sent into exile,[3] but his *Li Shao*, an elegy on patriotism, ranks as one of the greatest Chinese poems. Zuo Qiu went blind[4] but still managed to write the *Histories of States*, an important historical record. Sun Zi,[5] who lost his kneecaps, wrote *The Art of Warfare*, the oldest and most distinguished book on warfare. Lü Buwei,[6] who was exiled in Sichuan, wrote *Lü's Spring and Autumn Annals*. Han Fei,[7] who was imprisoned in Qin, authored two books: *On Difficulties* and *Solitary Wrath*. Sima Qian,[8] who was made a eunuch, wrote *The Records of the Historian*, the book that started the tradition of Chinese biographical history. Gou Jian, the king of Yue,[9] slept on firewood and tasted gall to remind himself of his humiliation and to steel his determination to rid his country of invaders. He eventually realised his ambition.

The indomitable spirit shown by such people lived on through the centuries. In more recent times, it has manifest itself in the spirit of 'two bombs and one satellite',[10] the spirit of Wang Jinxi,[11] the spirit of the Chinese Women's Volleyball Team in the 1980s, the spirit of the Chinese Women's Football Team in the 1990s and the indomitable spirit of Deng Xiaoping throughout his long career. Most importantly, it manifest itself in the energetic work of the Chinese people to reduce the gap between China and the developed countries and to promote China's rejuvenation.

The spirit of humanity

The spirit of humanity is the criterion by which Chinese people live. Over thousands of years it was tempered and polished to reach a higher level, and is now the basis of morality and ethical values. What is humanity? When a student of Confucius asked this question Confucius replied, 'It is love for others.' According to Confucius, 'When you do five things for the world, you have humanity.' These five things are 'respect, tolerance, integrity, nimbleness, and favour'. When striving to establish oneself or accomplish something, one should help others to do likewise. In other words, 'Do unto others as you would have them do unto you.' The spirit of humanity advocated by Mo Zi[12] represented the zenith of such thinking. He and his followers advocated universal love and harmony, and a world in which 'the strong do not control the weak, the many do not frighten the few, the wealthy do not bully the poor, the noble do not scorn the humble, and the shrewd do not cheat the slow'. Mencius[13] considered that 'the heart of compassion, the heart of feeling ashamed of evil, the heart of courtesy and the heart to know right from wrong' were the starting points of humanity, justice, politeness and wisdom.

It is this spirit of humanity that over the centuries provided the Chinese nation with great cohesion and enabled the people to unite to advance social development and the Chinese civilisation.

The spirit of diligence

The spirit of diligence is what the Chinese nation has relied on to live in peace, create wealth and explore the unknown. Diligence includes diligence in learning, thinking, exploration and labour. Reading a book and not putting it down until it is finished is called diligence in learning. Being early to rise and late to bed for the sake of national prosperity is called diligence in government. Toiling and moiling in one's career is called diligence in labour. Diligence requires assiduity and enthusiasm, and neither is possible without the other. The sayings 'Learn broadly and commit yourself to ambition; consult often and think deeply', 'Efficiency comes only from diligence' and 'There is no royal road to learning but diligence' express the spirit of diligence upheld by the Chinese people since ancient times in the pursuit of personal and national betterment.

The spirit of exploration

Chinese philosophers and men of learning throughout the centuries have deemed it important to explore the unknown. The spirit of exploration refers to exploring laws of the universe and moral values, that is, understanding the value of life by seeking truth through the study of phenomena in nature and society. Studying nature was considered the starting point for cultivating oneself, putting one's family in order, running the local community and ensuring peace and security for the whole country. Such exploration was very meaningful. As Confucius said, 'I will not regret death at dusk if I have found the way at dawn.' Qu Yuan[14] never ceased his 'search upward and downward' for the way. The search was not limited to the natural sciences but also embraced philosophy, literature and art.

As a result of the spirit of exploration, great discoveries were made in the natural sciences, a field in which China led the world for millennia, and Chinese culture and art yielded rich fruits that have become treasures of global civilisation. Nowadays, this spirit is present in the policies and measures adopted to speed up China's development.

The spirit of creativity

The Chinese are a creative people, and the early evolution of their civilisation was accompanied by innovations in politics, economics, culture, and science and technology. In *China: Land of Discovery and Invention* (1986), Robert Temple states that of the major inventions in the world of today, more than half might have originated from ancient Chinese civilisation, and that modern agriculture, navigation, the oil industry, meteorology, firearms, aeronautics and steam power owe much to Chinese inventions. While the rigidity of the feudal system and then leftist ideology later constrained the spirit of creativity, from the late 1970s the policy of reform and opening up to the outside world enabled its resurgence, and since then there has been considerable new evidence of the creative and innovative minds of the Chinese people.

The spirit of moral integrity

The spirit of moral integrity is a strong, noble and vital force. The ancient Chinese believed that life could not be precious unless it was endowed with morality and justice, and idealists over the centuries thought that the essence of existence consisted of morality and integrity. Wang Fuzi's ideas, "life can only be precious when life carries righteousness" and "life can be sacrificed when righteousness supports life" are the agglomeration of such a spirit. Mencius passed a saying down through the ages "wealth does not allow for extravagance, poverty does not allow for lowliness, and force does not allow for submissiveness", which is a classic criterion for the spirit of moral integrity of the Chinese nation. Wen Tianxiang, a well-known national hero, sacrificed his life to realise that 'As death befalls all men alike, I will keep a loyal heart to make a name in history.' It is now a milestone in the spirit of moral integrity. The past five millennia have produced numerous people with lofty ideals and a strong sense of integrity over all periods of time. Some of these idealists remained righteous and incorrupt, serving the people to the end of their lives. Some risked their lives for the general good. Some died in action, fearlessly laying down their lives for a just cause. The spirit shown by these people was passed from generation to generation and encouraged the Chinese nation to conquer injustices. It was this spirit that fired the reformers discussed in this book.

The spirit of patriotism

The spirit of patriotism is deeply embedded in the Chinese people and is the source of national cohesion. Honouring and loving one's country means defending it and making it prosper, and the Chinese people have never shrunk from these duties. For thousands of years, the heroic deeds of numerous patriots have been on the lips of every household. The words of some of these patriots have been recorded for posterity, including those of Jia Yi[15] ('Put the country before the family and the public before the individual'), Zhuge Liang[16] ('Serve the people till the end of life'), Fan Zhongyan, ('Care about the world first and enjoy comfort afterwards'), Gu Yanwu[17] ('Everyone is duty-bound to help when the country is in peril'), Yue Fei[18] ('What else can one do but give one's life for one's country?'), Lin Zexu[19] ('If it benefits the country to give my life to it, how can I care about the risks involved?'), Qiu Jin[20] ('I do not care about the success or failure of what I do, only about shedding blood to repay my motherland'), Sun Yat-sen[21] ('Take the people out of fire and trouble') and Deng Xiaoping ('I am the son of the Chinese people, and I love my motherland and my people deeply'). The same spirit of patriotism has been behind the Chinese people's determination to advance China economically and socially over last two and a half decades.

The spirit of revolution

The spirit of revolution is the sword with which the Chinese people have resisted brute force from outside and evil elements within. China has a long history of revolution. From ancient times onwards, peasant uprisings against oppression shattered the foundation of the ruling classes and forced them to compromise or give way to new dynasties. For example, the Qin Dynasty was ended by the Chen Sheng and Wu Guang Uprising,[22] and the largest peasant uprising in the history of China led to the establishment of the Kingdom of Heavenly Peace[23] in the late Qing period. Subsequently, the Qing dynasty was further weakened by the Huanghuagang Uprising[24] and brought to an end by the Wuchang Uprising.[25] In the 1920s, the communist revolutionaries waged a bloody civil war against the nationalist Kuomintang. In the 1930s and earlier 1940s, both sides fought against the Japanese invaders, but after the surrender of Japan in 1945 civil war returned. The nationalists were defeated in 1949 and the People's Republic was born. However, the spirit of revolution lived on and was eventually channelled into the peaceful drive to rejuvenate China.

The spirit of reform

Reform has a long-standing tradition in China. To promote social growth and national prosperity, over the centuries numerous reformers emerged to oppose conservatism. As Shang Yang[26] put it during the Warring States period, 'We do not have to follow the ancient blindly if what we do benefits the state, or its rituals if what we do benefits the people.' Han Fei[27] was another ardent advocate of reform. He believed that the world had to be changed and that 'saints do not die for the ancient or their rigid laws'. Later, Chao Cuo carried out reform during the Western Han dynasty, Wang Anshi[28] during in the Northern Song dynasty and Zhang Juzheng[29] during the Ming dynasty. More recently, the Wuxu Reforms[30] of 1898 became a household story.

Some reformers advocated the reform of land ownership and the abrogation of hereditary rule. Some proposed the weakening or abolishment of vassalage in order to centralise state power. Some reformed taxation to relieve social conflict. Others introduced reforms to strengthen the nation and the army. Regardless of their success or failure, their efforts both reflected the spirit of the times and had far-reaching effects on later generations. The current reforms, aimed at the establishment of a socialist market economy, are unparalleled in scale and depth. Moreover, the spirit of reform has never been so deeply rooted in ordinary hearts or shown such great vitality.

The spirit of opening up to the outside world

China's opening up to the outside world has been a long process. The idea of 'coordination with ten thousand lands' can be found in ancient texts and refers to the coordination of international relations and infiltration of other lands. Confucius's saying that 'when other lands do not yield, naturalise them with culture and virtue so that they will come to you of their own accord' also refers to opening up. Mo Zi[31] advocated universal love and condemned offensive war, preferring instead the solution of international conflict through peace. However, in the Han and Tang dynasties, when China was powerful, rulers tended to look down on the rest of the world, which was perceived as backward in terms of economics, science and technology. Hence, China failed to recognise the value of learning from other countries and conducting economic exchanges with them. Although trade via the Silk Road was economically profitable and culturally significant as an East–West bridge, it was regionally restricted and temporary. The seven voyages made by Zheng He[32] were intended purely to show off China's prowess to the rest of the world.

Later, when Western industrial and naval power grew, the Chinese realised that their country was falling behind. Feng Guifen, a thinker, began to call for 'learning from the West to make China strong', and Wei Yuan[33] suggested that China should 'deal with foreigners with the skills of foreigners'. Eventually, China accepted the need to absorb Western advances in science, technology and academic thinking. Since the end of 1970s, globalisation and the necessity of bringing the economy out of the doldrums have made opening up one of China's main policies. In this new era, the spirit of opening up to the outside world has given great vitality to China's economic and social growth, and has brought historical changes to the country.

To sum up, for more than five millennia the Chinese nation has evolved a national spirit to suit the requirements of the times and the social development of the people. It is this spiritual force that has given impetus to China's rejuvenation in recent decades, and will continue to inspire the Chinese people to strive for an even better future.

7
The Momentum that Stemmed from Globalisation

There can be little doubt that globalisation has played a part in the course taken by China in recent decades. Since the late 1970s, globalisation has acted as both stress and dynamics in powerfully pushing Chinese people to rise and dedicate all their efforts to changing China's unfortunate situation of stagnation and backwardness, and to strive for their desired future. What precisely is globalisation? The most widely accepted definition is that by David Held and his coauthors: globalisation is 'a process (or set of processes) which embodies a transformation in the spatial organisation of social relations and transactions – assessed in terms of their extensity, intensity, velocity and impact – generating transcontinental or interregional flows and networks of activity, interaction, and the exercise of power'.[1] Here, flows refers to the movement of goods, people, symbols, tokens and information across space and time, and networks refers to regularised or patterned interactions between independent agents, nodes of activity or holders of power. This definition is beneficial in distinguishing globalisation from the more spatially limited processes of regionalisation and internationalisation. The globalisation process can be analysed according to four spatial–temporal dimensions: the extensiveness of the networks of global relations and connections, the intensity of flows and levels of activity within these networks, the velocity or speed of global flows, and the impact of these phenomena on particular communities.[2] In short, globalisation is a process in which countries and regions are drawn into a global system that affects all aspects of human life, and what happens in one part of the world affects or shapes what happens in many other places.

Politically, globalisation means that 'the national state is less able to control the agenda than it was in the past'.[3] Economically, the advantages enjoyed by advanced countries are being shared with an ever-increasing number of others, including developing countries and those in transition. Socially, the diffusion of sophisticated information technology and other new means of communication has brought about a 'reordering of the time and distance in our life'[4] or a 'time–space compression'[5] that enables global social relations.

It is generally agreed that economic globalisation began in the mid-twentieth century and gathered momentum from the 1970s. The extent to which countries have been affected by the phenomenon varies considerably, but the pressure for change has been felt most strongly by the most backward or stagnant economies. At the end of 1970s China, which had just emerged from the turmoil of the Cultural Revolution, was facing great pressure from the outside world, which was characterised by accelerating economic growth and increasing integration. What effect did this have on China's development? Did it precipitate the reform and opening-up processes? To what extent might it have benefited China's rejuvenation? These issues will be discussed in detail below.

This section first explores the problems China encountered prior to the 1980s and then how the pressure of globalisation pushed it to rectify its economic situation.

As discussed earlier, China occupied the leading position in economic and technological development for thousands of years. Between 1400 and 1800, when global trade focused strongly on Asia, China had huge export markets, particularly for silk, china and tea. In 1820, China's GDP was the highest in the world – 5.7 times that of Britain, 15.9 times that of the United States and 11.9 times that of Germany.[6] However, due to many social and other reasons, Chinese exports began to decline from the second quarter of the nineteenth century. According to Paul Bairoch, in terms of manufacturing production the Chinese economy reached it lowest point in the early 1900s and stagnated thereafter (Figure 7.1). In 1750, China accounted for one third of world manufacturing production, but in about 1870 it was overtaken by Britain, and then by the United States in 1890.[7] According to many scholars, the main reason for this decline was the shackling

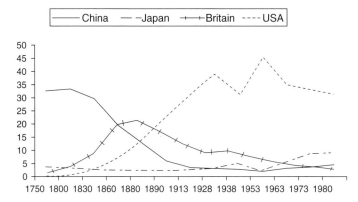

Figure 7.1 Share of world manufacturing production, major producers, 1750–1980 (per cent)

of China's outdated feudal system to the development of social productivity. China's feudal society lasted too long. In its final years the feudal political system, ideology and state operating mechanisms became ossified and inefficient. This, combined with autocracy and corruption, weakened the country economically, technologically and scientifically.

After the founding of the People's Republic there was some improvement but China's relative backwardness did not change fundamentally. There were three principal reasons for this. First, Soviet-style mandatory planning and centralisation were not suited to economic development. Second, political intervention in all economic activities restricted the development of the economy. Third, the lack of exchanges, cooperation and competition with other economies prevented China from absorbing capital, new technologies and managerial skills from the outside world.

The last of the above points returns us to the subject of globalisation, in which 'all aspects of [the] economy – raw materials, labour information and transportation, finance, distribution, marketing – are integrated or interdependent on a global scale'.[8] Thus, globalisation facilitates the movement of investment capital, lowers trade barriers, loosens or removes exchange controls and displaces public sector capital with private capital. History has shown that the more a country or region integrates itself into the world economy the more likely it is to accelerate its economic growth, and *vice versa*. A country's degree of global integration can be calculated according to the Globalisation Index: 0–1 (low), 1–2.5 (medium) and 2.5–5 (high).[9] Highly integrated countries include Singapore (4.25), the United States (4.12) and Hong Kong (3.63), while Germany (2.33), South Korea (1.92), Japan (1.62), Britain (1.52) and France (1.39) fall into the medium range. In 1998, China's Globalisation Index was just 0.26, and this had been a result after twenty years of hard catching-up efforts.

While China's economy stagnated in the early 1970s, other economies in the region forged ahead, including those of Japan, which became an economic superpower in a very short period, and the Asian Tigers. By the end of the Cultural Revolution, the Chinese economy was on the brink of bankruptcy and per capita GNP was much smaller than that of the more successful countries and regions around China in Asia (Table 7.1).

As is well known, one of the principal engines of globalisation was the rapid development and diffusion of technology, especially information technology, which enabled people to compare the situation in their own country with that in others. It also increased the cultural and economic influence of the advanced countries. Inevitably both factors put great pressure on the governments of backward countries. In the late 1970s, China was just beginning to fall into this difficult position.

Table 7.1 Per capita GNP and GDP annual growth rate, selected Asian countries, and regions, 1960–78

	Per capita GNP 1978 (US $)	GDP annual growth rate (per cent)	
		1960–70	*1970–78*
China	230	5.0	6.0
Malaysia	1 090	6.5	7.8
South Korea	1 160	8.5	9.7
Taiwan	1 400	9.2	8.0
Hong Kong	3 040	10.0	8.2
Singapore	3 290	8.8	8.5

Source: World Bank (1980), pp. 110–13.

First, the rapidly strengthening economic power of the developed countries and regions was putting heavy pressure on China as any enlargement of the gap between them and China would further weaken China's competitive power and international status. Second, China's Soviet-style mandatory planning and economic isolation had proved to be highly detrimental to economic growth and therefore needed to be reconsidered. Third, if the gap between China and the more developed economies was not reduced soon, people's living standards would suffer and this could result in their losing confidence in the political system and the legitimacy of the regime. This would further weaken China's international status and delay reunification with Hong Kong, Macao and Taiwan.

Because of the above it was essential to absorb capital, new technologies and managerial skills from developed countries and to join competition in the global arena. As Deng Xiaoping put it, 'We summed up our historical experiences, and an important reason why China got bogged down in...stagnation and backwardness in the past was closing the country to international exchanges. Experience has proved that to engage in economic reconstruction while closing the country makes it impossible to achieve success.'[10] China's development is inseparable from the world. Therefore, when the authorities discussed China's future development strategy at the end of 1978, they gave the top priority to opening up the economy. Details of the subsequent economic measures are provided in Chapters 4 and 5.

It has been two and a half decades since the commencement of China's reform and opening-up programmes. In retrospect, it is reasonable to assume that the massive economic success being enjoyed by other countries and regions as they rode the wave of globalisation spurred China's policy makers to rethink their policies and abandon the outdated theoretical doctrines and patterns of decision making that were shackling China's development. Opening up to the outside world would also allow China to obtain international resources to promote its modernisation drive, including foreign capital, advanced technology and the latest theories and practices in economics, management, law and the social sciences.

From 1993, China was continuously the top developing-country recipient of foreign direct investment, and in 2002 it overtook the United States to become the top world recipient. Of the 500 major transnational companies, more than 400 have invested or set up enterprises in China. China has not only been investors' first choice but also the 'safe island' of world investment.[11] This, together with other aspects of China's impressive economic growth in the last quarter century, offers convincing evidence that globalisation has played an important part in China's development and rejuvenation.

8
The Dynamics of China's Future Development

Our exploration of the dynamics of China's rejuvenation inevitably raises questions about China's future. Can it sustain its effective policies and adopt new ones to further its modernisation drive? Will it be able to maintain the social stability needed to complete its ambitious development programme? Will it be able to sustain its progress towards complete national rejuvenation? To answer these questions, this chapter considers the conditions for and foundations of further development, and the likely dynamics of future development.

China's rapidly strengthening economic power as the basis of further development

As discussed in Chapter 2, China has experienced unprecedentedly rapid economic growth and is now one of the largest economies in the world in terms of GDP.[1] According to the index created by the Institute of World Economics at the Shanghai Academy of Social Science to measure economic power (EP), and setting the US index at 100, in 2000 China's index was 56.4 and it occupied fifteenth place in the ranking of the world's most powerful economies, compared with twenty-fifth in 1990. In 2002, its GDP exceeded 10 trillion yuan for the first time, and its growth rate reached 8 per cent. Contracted foreign direct investment (FDI) amounted to $82.768 billion and the amount actually used came to $52.743 billion, more than anywhere else in the world. Imports and exports exceeded $600 billion, placing

China fifth in the world ranking, and its foreign exchange reserves added up to close on $300 billion.[2]

China's rapidly growing economic power has changed the balance of trade in Asia. According the *New York Times*,[3] 'The United States still remains an essential trading partner for Asian countries but is becoming somewhat less important in the face of China's rise.' This has been reported 'as the beginning of an inescapable process of China replacing the United States as the dominant power in Asia'.[4] In short, after 20-odd years of exceptional development, China has turned itself into quite a strong economic power, thus providing a firm foundation for its future development.

In the absence of unexpected economic shocks at home or abroad, it is predicted that China's economic growth will remain above 7 per cent until at least 2010, GDP will quadruple by 2020 (Table 8.1) and China will overtake Germany to become the world's third largest economy in 2012, with the United States and Japan occupying first and second places respectively.[5]

Table 8.1   Predicted growth of GDP, China, 2000–29

	GDP (billion US $)	Annual increase (%)
2000	1080.0	8.9
2001	1161.0	7.5
2002	1248.1	7.5
2003	1341.7	7.5
2004	1442.3	7.5
2005	1550.5	7.5
2006	1666.8	7.5
2007	1791.8	7.5
2008	1926.2	7.5
2009	2070.7	7.5
2010	2226.0	7.5
2011	2370.7	6.5
2012	2524.8	6.5
2020	4178.3	6.5
2025	5460.9	5.5
2026	5761.2	5.5
2029	6765.1	5.5

Note: Calculated according to prices in 2000 and the average dollar–yuan exchange rate in 1998–2000.
Source: Xu (2002).

The backing of the people

The confidence of Chinese people in their future has been strengthened enormously by China's remarkable economic growth and social development over the past two and a half decades. They have every reason to believe that, through unceasing hard effort, they can enable China to catch up with the developed countries in the not too distant future and build a dynamic new society.

Moreover, they have great confidence in the current government and its ability to make appropriate institutional arrangements and state affairs to the benefit of the people. Although much still needs to be done to perfect institutional frameworks, policies and so on, the public trust in China's leaders has profound significance for the country's future development.

Finally, the cohesion of the Chinese nation is another important point in favour of further development. For thousands of years China has been more successful than any other country in unifying its hundreds of millions of people both politically and culturally.

The stable transfer of power

As discussed briefly in Chapter 5, in the 1980s, steps were taken to abolish the traditional system of lifetime tenure and provisions were made for older leaders to retire and hand over the reins of power to a younger generation. In 1989, a group headed by Jiang Zemin took over from Deng Xiaoping and continued to direct the reform programme. The most recent leading group, headed by Hu Jingtao and Wen Jiabao, is also unswervingly adhering to the reforms. This history of peaceful power transfers indicates that China will sustain its policies and continue its modernisation drive. Although the new group has only been in power for a short time, it has earned a reputation abroad for 'being conscientious in its work' and having a 'spirit of realism'.[6] For instance, Reuters News Agency considers that the firm measures Hu adopted for handling the SARS outbreak demonstrated his ability to resolve practical problems.[7] Moreover, a recent public opinion poll conducted in Beijing, Shanghai, Guangzhou, Chongqing and Nanjing found that more than 80 per cent of interviewees were satisfied or relatively satisfied with the government's work in fighting SARS and 76.4 per cent stated that their confidence in the government had increased.[8]

The experiences learnt from China's reform practices

In the course of its modernisation drive, China has acquired valuable experiences that can guide future development.[9] First, the Chinese people have acquired a greater understanding of the country's targets, how to accomplish them and the type of government needed by China. Second, the people have learnt that if China is to compete in the global market it will be essential to be constantly innovative, theoretically and practically. Third, the government has realised that it will be crucial to keep economic development as its central task and to solve existing problems effectively, as without sustained development it could lose the support of the people and its legitimacy.

Fourth, it is essential to persist unswervingly in reform and opening up, and keep developing and improving the socialist market economy. Fifth, it is also essential to develop a socialist democracy that attaches equal importance to the creation of material civilisation, spiritual civilisation and political civilisation by combining the rule of law with the rule of virtue. Sixth, it is imperative to be painstaking in balancing reform; development and stability are prerequisites for both reform and development. Also, it is necessary to balance the intensity and speed of reforms with the people's ability to accept change. This means moving step by step rather than introducing radical reforms or even using shock therapy, as has happened in some economies in transition.

Seventh, attention has to be paid to dealing with the relationships between the efficiency of economic development and social equity, and between encouraging those who have the potential to become rich ahead of others and common prosperity of the whole society. Actually, these are the issues concerning how to speed up economic development and how to handle value distribution justly. In practice, China persisted in the principle of stressing first the priority of efficiency following the market laws in production and primary income distribution, by which creativity and industriousness in people's works would be encouraged. Income redistribution should then be carefully conducted through the relevant means, such as taxing and social security policies, and so on. In so doing, due consideration should be given to both the equity of opportunity and the actual equality by which to maintain social stability and to keep the harmonious development of society.

As a very large country, both in territory and population, China's economic development levels and natural conditions vary from region to region. Therefore, it is impossible for all regions and all people to get rich together simultaneously and to the same extent. Accordingly, China's experience is, as Deng Xiaoping advocated at the outset of the reform, to allow and encourage some regions and some people with appropriate conditions to get rich ahead of others, and then to promote and realise common prosperity for the whole of society gradually.

Eighth, it is vital to combine the spirits of theoretical innovation and the strategy of adopting safe practical measures. China's reform and opening-up are completely new undertakings. They should therefore proceed boldly but carefully in accordance with the prevailing conditions governing the development of productive forces and society. In so doing, theoretical innovation is crucial, without which it would be impossible for China to achieve any development. Past practice showed that the emancipation of the ideology and the theoretical breakthroughs often serve as the preconditions of reform.

Furthermore, while trying to bring the role of market mechanisms into full play in economic construction, China adhered to paying great attention to conducting macro control by offering necessary policy guidance and institutional frameworks. To achieve this, China's government adopted a full range of bold but safe measures, such as 'double-track system' policy (that is, two kinds of policies) on the same issue in order to conduct more comparisons, to experiment first and popularise later when implementing policies in order to reduce risk, and so on. In short, to carry effective reform forward step by step whilst avoiding social shock waves and reducing the risks inherent in the reform where possible.

Finally, it is crucial for China to adhere to an independent peace foreign policy, doing all it can to safeguard world peace. For 20 or so years, China has attached great importance to the defence of state sovereignty and security, and to try its utmost to develop friendly relations with other countries. It opposes hegemony and power politics, and favours the establishment of a fair and rational new international political and economic order. In recent decades, the international situation has been highly volatile and complicated. However, China has maintained its presence of mind and called for justice, fair play and cooperation through competition, based on mutual respect. This has not only strengthened China's international status but also attracted foreign investment to aid its drive for modernisation.[10] Moreover, in negotiating for the return of Hong Kong and Macao to China, dealing with the bombing of the Chinese embassy in Yugoslavia, the Sino-US plane collision, and bringing the long and difficult negotiations for China's entry to the WTO to a successful conclusion, China has displayed a proper diplomatic demeanor, courage and wisdom, thereby improving its international relations and creating the right climate for its future development.

A clearly defined target for living standards

The leadership's social goal is to build a *xiaokang* society. The concept of *xiaokang* comes from *The Book of Song*, China's most ancient poetry collection. Its literal meaning is 'moderately well-off'; that is, it refers to a society that is less affluent than well-off but free from want. When China initiated its reforms in 1979, Deng Xiaoping referred to *xiaokang* as the goal to be attained by the end of the twentieth century. In 1984 he elaborated on this, saying '*xiaokang* means that, by the end of this century, our per capita gross domestic product will reach US$800'.[11] Although this goal was reached and then exceeded, in 2002 Jiang Zemin reported that people's living standards were still at a low level and very uneven.[12] At the time, China's per capita GDP was $1000, compared with a minimum of $3000 in developed countries.

However, the current targets are to quadruple per capita GDP of 2000 to $3000 by 2020, and to raise other social development indices by improving democracy, advancing science and education, enriching the Chinese culture, fostering social harmony and generally improving the fabric of people's lives.[13] In other words, the *xiaokang society*, which is much better than *xiaokang* life, will combine the creation of material civilisation and spiritual civilization, political civilisation and ecologic civilisation harmoniously at a high level.

Twenty-four years ago, Deng's promise of a *xiaokang* living standard motivated the people to work hard to build up the economy. The new goal of building an even better-off society with high overall standards is again encouraging the people to put their all into the modernisation programme, which will turn 'China into a strong, prosperous, democratic and culturally advanced socialist country by the middle of this century'.[14]

Ideological emancipation

Looking back over the history of the past 25 years, one can see that the ideological emancipation that has taken place in the course of the reforms has considerably benefited China's development. Furthermore, it is likely to continue to do so in the future. This emancipation has been in four main areas. As discussed in Chapter 5, the first was to replace the cult of personality and doctrinairism with the ideological practice of seeking truth from fact.

The second and third were to break away from the doctrines of mandatory central planning and state ownership of the means of production. For a long time people continued to think that, by definition, socialism meant public ownership and a planned economy, and they worried that the reforms constituted a move towards capitalism. While they liked the idea of greater freedom, they involved themselves in endless arguments about the dividing line between socialism and capitalism. For some, only state ownership could ensure the country's development because the private sector was unreliable and perhaps even dangerous for society. However, when the household responsibility system was phased in to replace the communes (see Chapter 4), people's attitudes began to change, first in the countryside and then in the cities. Nowadays, many people have their own enterprises, own shares in state enterprises, and have their own houses and cars.

The fourth ideological emancipation was the CPC's new decision (of 2002) to 'keep pace with the times', and to serve the interests of all the Chinese people rather than just the working class. For instance, the recruitment of new party members, according to the new party constitution membership, would no longer be restricted to 'workers, farmers, intellectuals, servicemen and cadres, but would henceforth include advanced elements of other social strata who accept the party's programme and constitution, work for the realisation of the party's line and programme ... and meet the qualifications of party membership ... in order to increase the influence and rallying force of the party in society at large'.[15] Since then, the idea of keeping pace with the times has been a key factor in both policy making and social development.

The ideological changes discussed above have provided the backbone for the reforms and now constitute a solid theoretical and ideological foundation for China's further progress.

Membership of the World Trade Organization

After 15 years of hard bargaining, China joined the WTO at the end of 2001. China's acceptance as an equal member of the world economic community marked the coming of age of its economy and heralded a number of economic benefits and institutional changes.

Better conditions and motivation for foreign trade and foreign investment

By joining the WTO, China has become a full player on the international economic stage and a participant in the making of trade rules and the handling of trade disputes. More importantly, WTO membership has opened up new opportunities for Chinese exports and inward flows of foreign investment, thus boosting the development of the economy.

China's membership of the WTO, together with its stable political environment and rapidly growing economy have made it very attractive to foreign investors and traders. In 2002, just a year after joining the WTO, exports had increased by 22.3 per cent to reach $325.57 billion, and imports amounted to $295.22 billion, a rise of 21.2 per cent over the 2001 figure. In the process, China overtook Britain to become the world's fifth largest exporter, behind the United States, Germany, Japan and France.[16]

The same year, FDI reached unprecedented heights:[17] 34 171 new foreign enterprises were set up, an increase of 30.72 per cent over the previous year; contracted FDI reached $82.768 billion (an increase of 19.62 per cent); and actual FDI rose to $52.743 billion (an increase of 12.51 per cent). It has been predicted that FDI will amount to $100 billion in 2005,[18] double the 2002 figure.

WTO membership will ultimately lead to the removal of protectionist measures and the breaking up of monopolies in certain industries, resulting in a market system that is open and competitive.

The latter will be essential if China is to prosper in the global market.

Furthering institutional changes

The terms of WTO membership required thousands of China's ministerial and local government rules and regulations to be amended or annulled. For instance, in Shanghai there were some 2027 administrative procedures relating to local economic activities, more than 1000 of which have had to be abolished; the State Commission of Economy and Trade has had to annual 13 ministerial regulations; and 113 other ministerial regulations have had to be examined, many of which will be annulled or amended. Meanwhile, new regulations have been drawn up to regulate concessionary-operated commercial businesses, foreign-invested commercial enterprises and direct sales by foreign-invested enterprises, among other things.[19] These efforts will no doubt benefit China's administrative and economic efficiency in the future.

WTO membership has also prompted improvement of governmental policy making, policy implementation, and transparency. In the past, documents prepared by the various government commissions, ministries and departments were passed on to subordinate departments and enterprises on a 'need to know' basis, other general government bodies and enterprises being denied access to them. However, upon WTO accession this situation changed immediately. For instance, the Commission of Economy and Trade now publishes a publicly available bulletin on its policies, regulations, rules, activities and so on.

With the approval of the State Council, a number of new functional departments has been set up, such as the Bureau for Investigating Industrial Damage, the Bureau of Fair Trade and the Antidumping Consultation Service Centre of the Chinese Car Industry Association.[20] Furthermore, in order to improve local governments' management approach and efficiency, and to ensure democratic and systematic decision making, five cities have been selected to take part in an experimental programme[21] in which the administrative system will be divided into three areas: policy making, an executive branch and a supervisory branch. Each will function separately but they will collaborate in the fulfilment of local and governmental missions.

To sum up, it is obvious that WTO membership has given impetus both to China's economic growth and to the institutional reforms needed to ensure its continued economic and social development.

The international environment

China's development will continue to benefit from the general improvement of the international environment. The past ten or so years have shown that multipolarisation and economic globalisation are conductive to world development and stability. Although 'the old international political and economic order, which is unfair and irrational, has yet to be changed fundamentally; uncertainties affecting peace and development are on the rise; traditional and non-traditional threats to security are intertwined; the scourge of terrorism is more acutely felt; hegemony and power politics have new manifestations; and local conflicts triggered by ethnic or religious differences and border or territorial disputes have cropped up from time to time',[22] the general tendency is still towards peace and development because this is in the fundamental interest of all nations.

The world has recognised and welcomed China's growing international status, and views its rejuvenation as beneficial to the progress of human society. Furthermore, China's rise is not seen as a threat to the world order, as confirmed by a public opinion poll conducted in the United States in 2002.[23] Moreover, Roche Stephen, chief analyst at Morgan Stanley, has stated that China is helping to alleviate sluggishness of the global economy.[24]

China's diplomatic relations with other countries are also improving, to the benefit of China's further development. Sino-American relations are now defined as 'constructive cooperation', the Sino-Russian Treaty of Neighbourly Relations and Cooperation has boosted collaboration between China and Russia, and Sino-European relations are strengthening considerably, unlike relations between some European countries and the United States. Closer to home, China is also making a great effort to cement its ties with neighbouring Asian countries and to promote regional cooperation. For instance, through the Shanghai Six Countries Organisation, it built up a good relations with the countries around its northern border. Also, it has built up good relations with the Association of Southeast Asian Nations (ASEAN). Finally, China has a tradition of cooperation with other Third World countries, and recently mutual understanding and trust have increased and mutual help and support have strengthened. These relationships will be very important in providing China with support for its continuing drive for modernisation.

As this book has shown, China is now full of vim and vigour and looking forward to an even better future. In the past two and a half decades, it has extricated itself from a very difficult situation and brought about a national rejuvenation, thanks to the people's trust in and support of the government, the fruitful policies and enterprising spirit of the reformers, stable leadership, the impelling of the national spirit, and a favourable international environment.

Notes

1 Introduction

1. Guo (2002), pp. 1–15.
2. Bai (2002), pp. 40–7.
3. Government of China (2000a), pp. 54–5.
4. Bai (2002), p. 613.
5. A tael was a unit of currency whose value was equivalent to its ounce (or tael) weight in silver.
6. Government of China (2000a), pp. 54–8.

2 China's Rejuvenation

1. Quoted in *Xinhua Daily*, 29 January 2003, p. A4.
2. Ibid.
3. Quoted in Zhu and Ji (2003), p. B1.
4. Ibid.
5. 'China to Become Engine for World Economic Development', *Alexander's Gas & Oil Connections, News & Trends: E & SE Asia*, vol. 7, issue 22, 13 November 2002.
6. Jiang (2002), pp. 7–8.
7. Zhao (1999), pp. 290, 292.
8. *China Statistical Yearbook* (2002), p. 51.
9. *Economist* (2002), p. 25.
10. World Bank (1996), pp. 20, 173.
11. 'China Created "Best of the World" in Its Economic Development', *Jiefang Daily*, 19 September 2002.
12. 'China's Competitiveness Rises to 33rd Place in the world', *People's Daily*, 30 January 2003.
13. Government of China (2002e), p. 387.
14. Ibid., p. 388.
15. Zhu (2003); Government of China (2002d), p. 76.
16. Government of China (2002d), p. 75.
17. Zhu (2003); Government of China (2002d), pp. 386–90.
18. Government of China (2002d), p. 390; Zhu (2003), p. 2.
19. Hsü (2000), p. vii.
20. Ibid.
21. *New York Times*, 17 June 1998.
22. Lawrence H. Summers, former senior economist of the World Bank and Secretary of the Treasury in the Clinton administration. Quoted in Kristof (1993).

23. Hsü (2000), p. 981.
24. Ibid.
25. Hu and Wang (1998), p. 24.
26. *World Bank* (1997b), p. 3.

3 The Part Played by Chinese People in Bringing About Reforms

1. Liao and Zhuang (2001), p. 165.
2. Li (2002), p. 34.
3. Zhang (2002), pp. 9–10.
4. Government of China (2000b), p. 444.
5. Government of China (2000c), pp. 338–40.
6. Fang (1998), p. 4.
7. 'Sun Yefang – A Contemporary Economics Thinker Raised the Theory of "The Minimum and the Maximum"', www/xys/org/xys/ebooks/others/history/sun-yefang.text.
8. Gao (2000), pp. 385–9.
9. Xie (1999), pp. 669–70.
10. Liao and Zhuang (2001), pp. 460–1.
11. Li (1989), pp. 3–4.
12. Ibid., p. 131.
13. Shu (2001).
14. Ibid.
15. Li (1989), pp. 129–36.
16. Liao and Zhuang (2001), p. 194.
17. Chen (2000).
18. Ren (2000).
19. Jin (2001).
20. Yu (1998), p. 439.
21. The *Wenhui Bao* is the official newspaper of Shanghai. Since Shanghai was the base of the Gang of Four during the Cultural Revolution, the *Wenhui Bao* became one of the main vehicles for their propaganda.
22. Yu (1998), p. 440.
23. Zhang Chunqiao was one of the Gang of Four, a permanent member of the Politburo, Vice-Premier of the State Council and First Secretary of the Party Committee of Shanghai.
24. Guan and Li (2001), p. 349.
25. Liao and Zhuang (2001), pp. 431–2.
26. Guan and Li (2001), p. 357.
27. The three rural economic levels were the people's communes, the production brigades and the production teams.
28. Guan and Li (2001), p. 405.
29. Liao and Zhuang (2001), p. 472.
30. Chen (1998), pp. 224–30.
31. Li (2003), p. 2.
32. Ibid., pp. 2–3.
33. Ibid., p. 3.

34. Editorial note, 'The Road Towards Constitutional Government: Starting from Respecting the Constitution', *Southern Weekend*, 13 March 2003, p. 1.

4 The Part Played by Chinese Leaders Since 1978

1. Jiang Qing was Mao's wife and head of the Gang of Four.
2. Zhao (1996), p. 310.
3. Ma and Ling (1998).
4. Ibid., p. 42.
5. Ibid., p. 9.
6. Hsü (1990), p. 31.
7. Ibid.
8. Lin Biao (1907–71) joined the CPC in 1925, became defence minister in 1959 and vice-chairman of the Central Committee in 1969. He was killed in a plane crash in Mongolia on 13 September 1971 while fleeing to the USSR after an abortive coup attempt.
9. Jiang Qing (1914–91) was head of the Gang of Four and the wife of Mao Zedong since 1939. She was appointed deputy director of the leading group of Cultural Revolution of the Central Committee in 1966 and became a member of the Politburo in 1969. She was one of the most powerful political figures of the Cultural Revolution. For her evil deeds during the Cultural Revolution, she was arrested in October 1976 and subsequently sentenced to death (later commuted to life imprisonment).
10. He (1999), p. 269.
11. Xie (1999), pp. 761–2.
12. Liao and Zhuang (2001), p. 351.
13. He (1999), p. 269.
14. Liao and Zhuang (2001), p. 464.
15. He (1999), p. 270.
16. Lhasa is the capital of Tibet and the home of Tibetan Buddhism.
17. He (1999), p. 271.
18. Wang and Shun (1996), p. 6.
19. Deng Xiaoping (1980) 'The Present Situation and the Tasks Before Us', January 16, Speech at a meeting of cadres called by the Central Committee of the Communist Party of China. *Selected Works of Deng Xiaoping* (1975–1982) (Beijing: People's Press) p. 213.
20. Ibid., p. 214.
21. Liao and Zhuang (2001), pp. 587–8.
22. Ibid., p. 627.
23. *People's Daily Online*, 22 May 2003.
24. Li (1999a), p. 45.
25. Ibid., p. 46.
26. Zhang and Li (1997), pp. 71–2.
27. Jiao and Wang (1997), p. 69.
28. Jiang (1997), p. 14.
29. Li (1999a), p. 48.
30. Jiao and Wang (1997), p. 69.

31. Li (1999a), p. 50.
32. Zen (1999), pp. 45–6.

5 The Key Role of Deng Xiaoping

1. Quoted in Gong (1998).
2. 'Message to the Whole Party, the Whole Army and the People of All Nationalities Throughout the Country – From the Central Committee of the Communist Party of China, the Standing Committee of the National People's Congress of the People's Republic of China, the State Council of the People's Republic of China, the National Committee of the Chinese People's Political Consultative Conference, the Military Commissions of the Central Committee of the Communist Party of China and the People's Republic of China, 20 February 1997', *People's Daily*, 20 February 1997, p. 1.
3. 'Nations of World Send Condolences', *Beijing Review*, vol. 40, no.10, (1997), p. 27.
4. Ibid., p. 27.
5. Ibid., p. 28.
6. Nixon (1991), p. 332.
7. Hu (1998).
8. Deng (1984), p. 133.
9. Deng (1993), p. 373.
10. Ibid., p. 372.
11. Li (1999b), p. 11.
12. Deng (1982a), pp. 2–3.
13. Hsü (2000), p. 841.
14. Chen (1997), p. 12.
15. The term 'eating from the same rice pot', refers to the equal distribution of resources that prevailed before the reforms.
16. 'Deng Xiaoping's Discourse on Building Socialism with Chinese Characteristics', *People's Daily*, 18 January 1993.
17. Deng (1982b), pp. 12–13.
18. Peng (1997), p. 44.
19. Zhao (1996), p. 290.
20. Jiang (1997), pp. 9–10.
21. Zhao (1996), pp. 330–1.
22. Deng (1984), p. 140.
23. Shambaugh (1995), p. 77.
24. 'The General Architect of the Reform and Opening Up', *People's Daily*, overseas edition, 4 April 1997, p. 7.
25. Ibid.
26. Chen (1997), p. 9.
27. Khrushchev *et al.* (1974), p. 253.
28. Salisbury (1993), p. 328.
29. *People's Daily*, overseas edition, 6 March 1997, p. 7.
30. Chen (1997), p. 10.

31. Peng (1997), p. 44.
32. Chen (1997), p. 12.
33. Zhao (1996), p. 293. The Han, Wei and Jin dynasties followed the Qin, the first centralised feudal dynasty of China. The sentence 'I live in the Land of Peach Blossoms without knowing the Han dynasty or the dynasties of Wei and Jin' meant that he had been living in a place away from the turmoil of the world and was unaware of the changes that had taken place. His words actually implied his firm dismissal of the framework set out by Mao to affirm the achievements of the Cultural Revolution, which Deng considered to be an erroneous campaign.
34. Wang and Shun (1996), pp. 43–4.
35. Shambaugh (1995), p. 88.
36. Deng (1993), p. 372.
37. Chen (1997), p. 12.

6 The Fundamental Impetus Provided by the Chinese National Spirit

1. Quoted from Hsü (2000), p. vii
2. Wen was a leader in the late Shang dynasty (*ca* 1600–1100 BC) and father of the king of Wu, the founder of the Western Zhou dynasty (*ca* 1100–71 BC).
3. Qu Yuan (*ca* 340–278 BC) was a great patriot and poet. He lived during the Warring States period (when China was divided into several warring kingdoms) and was a high-ranking official in the state of Chu. At that time his homeland was under siege by another powerful state called Qin. The king of Chu poured scorn on Qu Yuan's suggestions for saving their country, officials subjected him to slander and he was eventually sent into exile. On the fifth day of the fifth lunar month, when he heard that the capital of Chu had fallen into enemy hands, he threw himself into the Miluo River (in present-day Hunan province) and drowned. Qu Yuan was deeply loved by the people. When villagers heard that he had thrown himself into the river they rushed to their boats to try to save him, but they were too late. Since then, boat races and the Dragon Boat Festival have been held on the fifth day of the fifth month to commemorate their rescue attempt.
4. Zuo Qiu, a historian, lived in the state of Lu during the Spring and Autumn period (770–476 BC).
5. Sun Zi was a great military strategist during the late Spring and Autumn period and author of *The Art of Warfare*, in which he summed up the experiences and lessons of many great battles and set down many important military thoughts. This work is the oldest and most distinguished book on warfare in Chinese history and is considered with pride by the Chinese nation. It has also attracted international attention and interest, as testified by its translation in to English, Japanese, German, French and Czech, among other languages.
6. Lü Buwei (?–235 BC) was prime minister of the state of Qin in the late Warring States period (475–221 BC).

7. Han Fei (*ca* 280–233 BC), also called Han Feizi, was a statesman and thinker during the late Warring States period.
8. Sima Qian was a great historian and scholar in the Han dynasty (206 BC–220 AD).
9. Gou Jian (496–465 BC) was king of the state of Yue during the late Spring and Autumn period. He became a household name because of the great perseverance and courage he exhibited when his country was defeated by the neighbouring state of Wu. He eventually defeated and annihilated the state of Wu.
10. The 'two bombs (atom and hydrogen) and one satellite' spirit relates to China's struggle to develop sophisticated defence technology in the face of a backward economy, weak industrial base and poor scientific and technological force, in order to resist the military threat of the big powers.
11. Wang Jinxi (1923–1970) was a famous national labour figure in the 1960s. He was called the 'Iron Man' and contributed greatly to the development of the Chinese petroleum industry.
12. Mo Zi, the reverent name of Mo Di (*ca* 468–376 BC), was a thinker and the founder of Mohism.
13. Mencius, the reverent name of Men Ke (*ca* 372–289 BC), was a famous Chinese philosopher and one of the greatest Confucian scholars.
14. See note 3.
15. Jia Yi (200–168 BC), a scholar and writer during the early Han dynasty, was famous for his *Fu* prose and political essays.
16. Zhuge Liang (formerly written as ChuKeh Liang) (181–231) was a statesman and strategist in the state of Shu. In Chinese folklore he came to be portrayed as the epitome of wisdom and resourcefulness.
17. Gu Yanwu (formerly written as Ku Yenwu) (1613–82) was a scholar and thinker during the late Ming and early Qing dynasties.
18. Yue Fei (1103–42) was a military commander during the Southern Song dynasty.
19. Lin Zexu (formerly written as Lin Tse-hsu) (1785–1850), a patriot and officer during the late Qing dynasty, banned the opium trade in Guangdong province.
20. Qiu Jin (1877–1907) was patriotic heroine, a resolute fighter for women's rights and a republican. She was killed by the Qing court in 1907.
21. Sun Yat-sen (1866–1925) led the 1911 revolution that overthrew the Qing dynasty and ended China's feudal society.
22. The Chen Sheng and Wu Guang Uprising (209 BC), also called the Dazexiang Uprising, was the first large-scale peasant uprising in China's history and brought about the collapse of the Qin dynasty.
23. Also called the Taiping Heavenly Kingdom (1851–1864).
24. The Huanghuagang Uprising of 27 April 1911 was led by Huangxing and others against the Manchu government.
25. The Wuchang Uprising (10 October 1911) marked the onset of the Revolution of 1911 (the Xinhai Revolution), led by Sun Yat-sen.
26. Shang Yang (*ca* 390–338 BC) was a statesman during the Warring States period. In about 356 BC in the state of Qin, he abolished the existing land

system and made land private, abolished the hereditary privileges of the nobility, encouraged a united farming and military effort, set up a unitary administrative system for the entire state, and unified weights and measures, thus laying the foundations for the state of Qin to become strong and eventually to unify China (221 BC).

27. Han Fei (formerly written as Han-Fei-Tzu) (*ca* 280–223 BC) was a statesman and thinker during the late Warring States period.

28. Wang Anshi (formerly written as Wang Anshih) (1021–1086) was writer, philosopher and statesman during the Northern Song dynasty. As prime minister, he initiated reforms to resolve social conflicts and a financial crisis.

29. Zhang Juzheng (formerly written as Chang Chu-cheng) (1525–1582) was statesman during the Ming dynasty.

30. The Wuxu Reforms (also called the Reform Movement of 1898, the year of Wuxu in Chinese chronology) were launched by Kang Youwei and other reformers under the auspices of Emperor Guangxu but suppressed by the Empress Dowager Cixi.

31. See note 12.

32. Zheng He (formerly written as Cheng Ho) (1371–1435) was a navigator and diplomat during the Ming dynasty.

33. Wei Yuan (1794–1857) was a thinker, historian and man of letters during the Qing dynasty.

7 The Momentum that Stemmed from Globalisation

1. Held *et al.* (1999), p. 16.
2. Ibid., pp. 16–17.
3. Parsons (1997), p. 235.
4. Giddens (1989), p. 519.
5. Harvey (1989), p. 240.
6. Hu (2002b), p. 6.
7. Bairoch (1982), pp. 296, 304.
8. Carnoy *et al.* (1993).
9. Hu (2002b), p. 7.
10. Deng (1993), p. 78.
11. Zhang and Huang (2003), p. 10.

8 The Dynamics of China's Future Development

1. *Economist* (2002), p. 24.
2. Zhang and Huang (2003), pp. 1, 18–19.
3. 'China Races to Replace US as Economic Power in Asia: NY Times', *People's Daily*, 28 June 2002.
4. Ibid.
5. Xu (2002).
6. Yue and Ren (2003), p. 2.
7. Reported in Ibid.
8. Gu (2003), p. 5.

9. These experiences are defined mainly according to speeches and reports by the leaders of The Communist Party, such as Jiang Zemin's 'Jiang sums up experiences over past 13 years' (*China Daily*, 11 August 2002) and Li Tieying's 'Great Practice and Successful Experience – in Celebration of the Twentieth Anniversary of the Third Plenary Session of the Eleventh Central Committee of the Communist Party of China' (*Social Science in China*, vol. 20, no. 3, 1999, pp. 16–21).

10. Jianrong (2000), p. 8.
11. Lu (2002), p. 4.
12. Jiang (2002), p. 21.
13. Ibid., p. 22.
14. Ibid.
15. Ibid., p. 65.
16. Wang and Zhang (2003), p. A4.
17. Zhang and Huang (2003), pp. 2–3.
18. Reyes (2001), quoted from Hu (2002a), p. 106.
19. Zhang and Huang (2003), p. 4.
20. Ibid., p. 5.
21. Yu (2003), p. 9.
22. Jiang (2002), p. 56.
23. Zhang and Huang (2003), p. 196.
24. 'China Is Contributing to the Global Economy', *Xinhua Daily*, 29 March 2003, p. 4.

References

Bai, Shouyi (ed.) (2002) *An Outline History of China* (Beijing: Foreign Languages Press).

Bairoch, Paul (1982) 'International Industrialization Levels from 1750 to 1980', *Journal of European Economic History*, vol. 11, no. 2.

Carnoy, M., Castells, M., Cohen, S. S. and Cardoso, F. (1993) *The New Global Economy in the Information Age* (Harrisburg, PA: Pennsylvania State University Press).

Chen, Jin (1997) 'Deng Xiaoping – A Great Man of the Century', *Chinese Youth*, no. 3.

Chen, Shaojing (2000) 'There are Still More New Secrets in the Unjust Case of Zhang Zhixin', *South Weekend*, 16 June.

Chen, Xuewei (1998) (ed.) *An Investigation of the Major Events Since the Third Plenary Session of the Eleventh Central Committee of CPC* (Beijing: Party School of CPC Centre Press).

China Statistical Bureau (2000) http://www.stats.gov.cn

China Statistical Bureau (2003) http://www.stats.gov.cn

China Statistical Yearbook – 2002 (2002) (Beijing: Statistical Publisher of China).

Deng, Xiaoping (1982a) 'An Opening Speech at the Twelfth National Congress of CPC, September 1, 1982', *Selected Works of Deng Xiaoping*, vol. 3 (Beijing: People's Press).

Deng, Xiaoping (1982b) 'Our Basic Stance on the Hong Kong Issue', in *Selected Works of Deng Xiaoping*, vol. 3. (Beijing: People's Press).

Deng, Xiaoping (1983) 'Current Situation and Task, (16 January 1980)', *Selected Works of Deng Xiaoping (1975–1982)* (Beijing: People's Press).

Deng, Xiaoping (1984) 'Emancipating the Mind, Seeking Truth from Facts, and Unifying Together with a Forward-Looking View', *Selected Works of Deng Xiaoping* (1975–82) (Beijing: People's Press).

Deng, Xiaoping (1993) 'The Main Points of the Speeches in Shenzhen, Zhuhai, and Shanghai', *Selected Works of Deng Xiaoping*, vol. 3 (Beijing: People's Press).

Economist (2002) *The Economist: Pocket World in Figures* (London: Profile Books).

Fairbank, John King and Goldman, Merle (1998) *China: A New History*, enlarged edn (Cambridge: Belknap Press of Harvard University Press).

Fang, Cai (1998) 'The Roles of Chinese Economists in Economic Reform', in *China Economy Papers*, published online by Asia Pacific Press, Canberra.

Gao, Jianguo (2000) *Making Firebrand with his Ribs – The Complete Biography of Gu Zhun*. (Shanghai: Shanghai Literature Press).

Giddens, A. (1989) *Sociology* (Oxford: Polity Press).

Gong, Yuzhi (1998) 'Three Great Changes and the Origin of Deng Xiaoping's Theory', *People's Daily*, 19 February, p. 10

Government of China (2000a) '*Human Rights in China*', in *White Papers of The Chinese Government*, vol. 1 (Beijing: Foreign Languages Press).

Government of China (2000b) 'Family Planning in China', in *White Papers of the Chinese Government* vol. 2 (Beijing: Foreign Languages Press).

Government of China (2000c) 'China's Population and Development in the 21st Century', in *White Papers of the Chinese Government*, vol. 3 (Beijing: Foreign Languages Press).

Government of China (2000d) 'Fifty Years of Progress in China's Human Rights', in *White Papers of the Chinese Government*, vol. 3 (Beijing: Foreign Languages Press).

Government of China (2000e) 'Progress in China's Human Rights Cause in 2000', in *White Papers of the Chinese Government*, vol. 3 (Beijing: Foreign Languages Press).

Gu, Zhaonong (2003) 'People's Observations: Analysing a Public Sentiment Poll in Five Cities', *People's Daily*, 3 June, p. 5.

Guan, Hong and Li, Xun (eds) (2001) *A Surging Centenary: A Record of One Century's China with Pictures and Essays: An Illustrated History of the Twentieth Century*. (Shanghai: Fudan University Press).

Guo, Peng (ed.) (2002) *China's Ancient History* (Beijing: Beijing Language and Culture University Press).

Harvey, David (1989) *The Condition of Postmodernity* (Oxford: Blackwell).

He, Qin (ed.) (1999) *A History of the People's Republic of China*, 2nd edn (Beijing: Higher Education Press).

Held, D., McGrew, A., Goldblatt, D. and Perraton, J. (1999) *Global Transformations: Politics, Economics and Culture* (London: Polity Press).

Hsü, Immanuel C. Y. (1990) *China Without Mao: The Search for A New Order*, 2nd edn (New York: Oxford University Press).

Hsü, Immanuel C. Y. (2000) *The Rise of Modern China*, 6th edn (New York: Oxford University Press).

Hu, Angang (ed.) (2001) *China: Fighting Against Corruption* (Hangzhou: Zhejiang People's Press).

Hu, Angang (ed.) (2002a) *Strategy of China* (Hangzhou: Zhejiang People's Press).

Hu, Angang (ed.) (2002b) *Globalisation Challenges Faced by China* (Beijing: Beijing University Press).

Hu, Angang and Wang, Yi (1998) *Pondering China: Nine Big Challenges Faced by China* (Shenyang: People's Publishing House of Liaoning).

Hu, Jingtao (1998) 'Speech at the Colloquium on the Twentieth Anniversary of the Discussion on the Criteria for Truth', *People's Daily*, 11 May.

Hu, Sheng (ed.) (1994) *A Concise History of the Communist Party of China* (Beijing: Foreign Language Press).

Huang, Jianrong (1999) *The Applicability of Policy-Making Theory in Post-Mao China* (Aldershot: Ashgate Publishing Ltd).

Huang, Jianrong (2000) 'The Dawn of China's Rejuvenation is Shining over the 21st Century', *People's Daily* (overseas edn), 8 April, p. 8.

Jiang, Zemin (1997) 'Holding High the Great Banner of Deng Xiaoping's Theory and Building Socialism with Chinese Characteristics in the Twenty-First Century', *Xinhua Monthly*, no. 10.

Jiang, Zemin (2002) 'Build a Well-off Society in an All-Round Way and Create a New Situation in Building Socialism with Chinese Characteristics', in *Documents of 16th National Congress of the Communist Party of China* (Beijing: Foreign Language Press).

Jiang, Zemin (2002) 'Jiang sums up experiences over past 13 years', *China Daily*, 11 August.

Jiao, Ran and Wang, Yanbing (1997) 'Great Theory, Magnificent Practice and Tremendous Changes: A Comment on China's Progress in Promoting the Socialist Market Economy', *Xinhua Monthly*, no. 9.

Jin, Feng, (2001) 'Wang Shenyou: Falling Down before the Muzzle of the "Two Whatevers" ', in *The Days We All Experienced* (Beijing: Beijing October Literature Press).

Kristof, Nicholas D. (1993) 'Entrepreneurial Energy Sets Off a Chinese Boom', *New York Times*, 14 February 1993.

Khrushchev, N. S. (ed.) Talbott, S. and Crankshaw, E. (1974) *Khrushchev Remembers: The Last Testament* (Boston: Little, Brown).

Li, Pu (2002) 'A Comment on the Most Depressing Page in the History of Beijing University', *Yan Huang Chun Qiu*, no. 10.

Li, Rui (1989) *A Memoir of the Lushan Meeting* (Beijing: Chunqiu Press, Hunan Education Press).

Li, Rui (2003) 'A Proposal for Reform of the Political System of Our Country', *Yan Huang Chun Qiu*, no. 1, p. 2.

Li, Shuzhi and Guo, Bing (2003) *The 16th Party Congress of the CPC and the Future of China* (Beijing: China Social Science Press).

Li, Tieying (1999a) 'The Setting Up and Breaking Through of the Theory of Socialist Market Economy', *Xinhua Digest*, no. 6.

Li, Tieying (1999b) 'Great Practice and Successful Experience – a Speech at the Celebration of the Twentieth Anniversary of the Third Plenary Session of the Eleventh Central Committee of the Communist Party of China', *Social Science in China*, vol. 20, no. 3.

Liao, Gailong and Zhuang, Puming (eds) (2001) *Chronicle of the People's Republic of China* (Zhengzhou: Henan People's Press).

Lieberthal, Kenneth (1995) *Governing China* (New York: W. W. Norton).

Lu, Xueyi (2002) 'Blueprint for a *Xiaokang* Society in China', *China Daily*, 3 December.

Ma, Licheng and Ling, Zhijun (1998) *The Belligerence of Thinkings: A Record of Ideological Emancipation for three times in Contemporary China* (Beijing: China Today Press).

Nixon, Richard (1991) 'China: the Aroused Giant', quoted in *The New Stars of Politics of the CPC in the Eyes of Foreigners* (Chengdu: Sichuan People's Press).

Parsons, W. (1997) *Public Policy: An Introduction to the Theory and Practice of Policy Analysis* (Cheltenham: Edward Elgar).

Peng, Mingbang (1997) 'A Legend of One Century', *Chinese Youth*, no. 3.

Ren, Zhongyi (2000) 'The Four Cardinal Principles Reconsidered', *Southern Daily*, 29 April.

Research Group on China's Modernization Strategy and the China Science Academy (2003) *Report on China's Modernization: 2003* (Beijing: Beijing University Press).

Reyes, Alejandro (2001) 'The Opportunity and Threat of China's Accession to the WTO', *World Link*, vols 3–4.

Ritcher, Frank J. (2002) 'China to become Engine for World Economic Development', *Alexander's Gas & Oil Connections, News and Trends: E & SE Asia*, vol. 7, no. 22, 13.

Salisbury, Harrison (1993) *The New Emperors, Mao and Deng: A Dual Biography* (London: HarperCollins).

Shambaugh, David (ed.) (1995) 'Deng Xiaoping: The Politician', in David Shambaugh, *Deng Xiaoping, Portrait of a Chinese Statesman* (Oxford: Clarendon Press).

Shu, Zhen (2001) ' "The Chronicle of Zhang Wentian's Life" ', Details of the Lushan Meeting', *Beijing Daily*, 15 January.

Temple, Robert K. G. (1986) *China: Land of Discovery and Invention* (Somerset: Haynes Publishing Group).

Wang, Ruipu and Shun, Qitai (eds) (1996) *Yearbook of the People's Republic of China*, vol. 4 (Beijing: Contemporary China Press).

Wang, Yiwei and Zhang, Jiehai (2003) 'The First Overseas Visit of China's New Head of State', *Southern Weekend*, 29 May, p. A4.

Water, M. (1995) *Globalisation* (London: Routledge).

World Bank (1980) *World Development Report* (Washington, DC: World Bank).

World Bank (1996) *World Development Report 1996: From Plan to Market* (New York: Oxford University Press).

World Bank (1997a) *China 2020: Development Challenges in the New Century* (Washington, DC: World Bank).

World Bank (1997b) *China Engaged: Integration with the Global Economy* (Washington, DC: World Bank).

World Bank (1999) *World Development Report 1999/2000: Entering the 21st century* (New York: Oxford University Press).

Xie, Chen (ed.) (1999) *Fifty Years of the People's Republic of China* (Beijing: Xinhua Press).

Xinhua Daily (2003) 'The World Economic Forum: China will be the Economic Growth Engine of the World', 29 January, p. A4.

Xu, Xianchun (2002) 'A Prediction of China's Economic Growth and its International Economic Status', *Economics Studies*, no. 3.

Yu, Huanchun (1998) '*People's Daily* and the Tiananmen Incident', in Xiao, Ke, Li Rui and Gong Yuzhi (eds) *The Political Movements I Experienced Personally* (Beijing: Central Compilation and Translation Press).

Yu, Mingsan (2003) 'Shenzhen's Experiment of Separating Administrative Power into Three Parts is in Progress', *Wenhui Daily*, 30 January.

Yue, Songlin and Ren, Yujun (2003) 'The World is Showing Great Concern for Hu Jintao's Visit', *Global Times*, 28 May, p. 2.

Zen, Peiyran (1999) 'The Achievements of China's Economy and Social Development over the Last Two Decades', *Xinhua Monthly*, no. 1, pp. 45–6.

Zhang, Jianping, Zhang, Yi and Mao, Xiaomei (2003) 'China is Still the Hot Country for Global Investment', *Wenhui Daily*, 15 May, p. 10.

Zhang, Jingsheng and Li, Anding (1997) 'Advance Steadily and Growth Speedily', *Xinhua Monthly*, no. 9, pp. 71–2.

Zhang, Xijin (2002) 'Ma Yinchu: Never Surrender to Criticisers who could not Convince People by Reasoning', *Yan Huang Chun Qiu*, no. 2, pp. 9–10.

Zhang, Youwen and Huang, Renwei (2003) *Report on China's International Status: 2003* (Shanghai: Shanghai Far-East Press).

Zhang, Zhuoyuan (1998) 'A General Review of China's Economic Reforms', *Economic Studies*, no. 3.

Zhao, Qizheng (ed.) (1999) *Development of the People's Republic of China over the Past 50 Years: A Collection of Graphs* (Shenyang, China: Shenyang Publishing House).

Zhao, Shigang (ed.) (1996) *The Changeable Economic Situation of the Republic* (Beijing: Economic Management Press).

Zhu, Rongji (2003) 'A Report on the Work of the Government, presented at the First Session of the 10th National People's Congress (NPC), 5 March 2003', *Wenhui Bao*, 20 March, p. 2.

Zhu, Yu and Ji, Ping (2003) 'The World is Fixing its Eyes on China', *Xinhua Daily*, 22 November, p. B1.

Index

aid-the-poor drive, 17
Annan, Kofi, 59
Anthropoid, the first, 3
April 5th movement,
    33–5, 72
astronomical records, 4

Bairoch, Paul, 84
big rice-pot, 64
Boxer Movement, 6
bronze culture, 3
bronze vessels, 3

cat theory, 72
Chao Cuo, 81
Chen Sheng and Wu Guang
    uprising, 80
Chi You, 3
China, 1, 2, 7
    accession to WTO, 96
    civilisation of, 2–4, 75
    economic competitiveness
        of, 15
    engine of world economy
        growth, 10
    epoch-making development
        of, 10–17
    fastest economic growth, 12
    FDI of, 14, 56, 96
    feudal political and
        bureaucratic system, 4
    foreign exchange reserves of,
        14
    foreign trade increase, 12
    four great inventions of, 4
    GDP of, 11, 18, 90
    institutional changes of, 97
    international relationships
        of, 98
    international status of, 17, 98

life expectancy, 17
    national rejuvenation of, 20
    power transition of, 69, 91
    production growth, 14
    reunification of, 64–5
    revolutionary change in, 18
    share of manufacturing
        production, 85
    sleeping giant, 75
    sporting achievements, 17
    socialist market system, 50
    written historical records
        of, 2
China's rejuvenation, 1,
    17, 99
    great impacts of, 2, 17–20
Chinese nation, 17, 82
    cohesion of, 77, 91
    rebirth of, 17
Chinese national spirit
    of creativity, 78
    of diligence, 77
    of exploration, 78
    of humanity, 77
    of moral integrity, 79
    of opening up, 81
    of patriotism, 79–80
    of reform, 81
    of revolution, 80
    of self-improvement, 76
Conference at Lushan
    Mountain (Lushan
    Meeting), 27
Confucian culture, 76
Confucius, 76–8, 81
constitutional government, 39
Cultural Revolution, 29, 32–3,
    42, 65, 86
    a historical catastrophe,
        41, 43

Daxi culture, 3
Deng Xiaoping, 8, 33–4, 47, 59,
    69, 70, 80, 87, 94
  chief architect of China's
    reform, 59, 65
  a great patriot, 71
  Mao's comments on, 70
  as the paramount leader, 41
  rehabilitation of, 36, 41, 65,
    71–2

egalitarian distribution
    system, 63
egalitarianism, 55, 64
Engel's coefficient
  of urban residents, 16
  of rural residents, 16
ethnic nationality policy, 46

family planning and population
    control, 22–3
Fan Zhongyan, 26
Feng Guifen, 82
Fiery Emperor, 3
First Opium War, 4

Gang of Four, 29–30,
    34–5, 42
General Line of Socialist
    Construction, 27
globalisation, 83, 85–7
Globalisation Index, 86
Gou Jian, 76
Great Leap Forward, 27, 29
Gu Yanwu, 80
Gu Zhun, 24–5

Han Fei, 76, 81
Held, David, 83
Hemudu culture, 3
heredity, 31
Hong Kong
  cession of, 4
  returned to China, 64–5
household consumption, 15–6
Hsü, Immanuel C. Y., 17–18

Hu Fuming, 25
Hu Jingtao, 91
Hu Yaobang, 48
Hua Guofeng, 41–2, 69
  legitimacy, 42
  wrong ideas of, 42
Huang Kecheng, 27–8
humanity, 77

ideological emancipations, 60–2,
    95–6
income, 15

Jia Yi, 80
Jiang Qing, 35, 42
Jiang Zemin, 65, 91

labour-intensive
    industrialisation, 27
Lantian man, 2
leftist mistakes, 28
leftist thinking, 67
Li Rui, 38
life expectancy, 17
Lin Biao, 29–30
Lin Zexu, 4, 80
Liu Shaoqi, 45
living standards, 16–17
Lü Buwei, 76

Ma Yinchu, 21
  'new population theories' of,
    21–2
Macau, 64–5
Major, John 59
macroeconomic control, 54
Majiapang culture, 3
Mao Zedong, 1, 27–9, 70, 73
market-driven economic
    system, 62
Marx, Karl, 59
Mencius, 77
metallurgy, 4
Mo Zi, 77, 81
multi-candidate election,
    system of, 38

Nanjing
    massacre in, 5
    Sino–British Treaty of, 4
Nanjing University, 34
Napoleon, 75
Needham, Joseph, 4

On Parentage (Yu Luoke), 31
one country, two systems, 64
opening up, 55, 87
Opium Wars, 4

paramount leader, 60
patriotism, 79–80
Peking man, 2
Peng Dehuai, 26–7
People's Commune Movement, 27
People's Democratic
    Dictatorship, 30
period of inaction, 69
personal cult, 29, 40
petty-bourgeois fever, 27
planned-economy cult, 95
post-Mao China, 43
    reform-oriented leadership in,
    41–56
purchasing power parity, 11–12

Qing government, 4
Qiu Jin, 80
Qu Yuan, 76, 78

redressing wrongs, 44–7
reform
    enterprise system, 53
    income distribution system, 55
    and opening-up, 19, 49
    ownership structure, 50–1
    political system, 38
    price system, 54
    rural economy system, 52
religion policy, 46
Ren Zhongyi, 30
Rightist opportunism, 28, 44, 45
rule by law, 39
rural industrialization, 52

SARS epidemic, 48, 91
seeking truth from fact, 28,
    60, 67
Shang Dynasty, 3
Shang Yang, 81
Shanghai Six Countries
    Organisation, 98
Shen Nong, 3
Shu Ape, 3
Silk Road, 82
Sima Qian, 76
Sino–Japanese Treaty of
    Shimonoseki, 6
socialism with Chinese
    characteristics, 62–3
socialist market economy,
    50, 92
Soviet-style mandatory
    planning economic
    system, 87
Special Economic Zones, 56
spheres of influence, 5
Sun Yat-sen, 80
Sun Yefang, 23–4
Sun Zi, 4, 76

Taiping Heavenly Kingdom
    Movement, 6
Taoism, 4
Taoist culture, 76
Thatcher, Margaret, 64
theoretical innovation, 93
Three Red Flags, 27
Three-Step Strategy, 68
Three Whethers, 61, 72
Tiananmen Square, 35–6
township enterprises, 52
transition, countries in, 11–12
transition economies, 11–13
Treaty of Nanjing, 6
truth, criteria, 25, 26, 37, 61
Two Whatevers, 42, 60, 69

Wan Li, 37
Wang Anshi, 81
Wang Fuzi, 79

Wang Shenyou, 32
Wei Yuan, 82
Wen Jiabao, 48, 81
Wen Tianxiang, 79
Wen King of Zhou, 76
World Economic Forum, 9
Wuchang Uprising, 80
Wuxu Reforms, 81

Xia Dynasty, 3
Xiaogang Village, 36–7
　household-contracted
　　responsibility system in, 36

Yangshou culture, 3
Yao Wenyuan, 34

Yellow Emperor, 3
　descendants of the Yellow and
　　Fiery Emperors, 3
Yeltsin, Boris, 59
Yu Luoke, 31
Yuanmou man, 2
Yue Fei, 80

Zhang Wentian, 27
Zhang Zhixin, 29–30
Zhao Zhiyang, 48
Zheng He, 82
Zhou Enlai, 34–5
Zhou Xiaozhou, 27–8
Zhuge Liang, 80
Zuo Qiu, 76